THE STORY OF BISHAM ABBEY

Portrait of Lady Hoby, Holbein School

THE STORY
OF
BISHAM ABBEY

PIERS COMPTON

Thames Valley Press
Maidenhead & Trowbridge
1973

This edition first Published by
Thames Valley Press, Maidenhead 1973
© Piers Compton

ISBN   0 90029 406 X

*Photoset and Printed
by Redwood Press Limited
Trowbridge, Wiltshire*

Preface

Some time ago I entertained Piers Compton and his wife to tea at Bisham Grange. We had mutual friends, but I had no idea that Piers was a writer.

In the course of conversation about the Abbey I said, "Oh, how I wish I could find someone to write a proper story about Bisham to correct all the many inaccurate references to its history, architecture and ghosts which are found in nearly all the books written about the Thames and its neighbourhood."

It later transpired that Piers thought the same, as the very next morning he telephoned me and offered to write the book himself.

It is strange that there are so few muniments in the possession of the family; but from such as I have got, and with much delving on his part, this book has taken shape.

We hope that historians, globe-trotters, local residents, and the many visitors making use of the sports and training facilities now available in the courses organised at Bisham will enjoy dipping into the past history of the Abbey which is so much a part of the history of England.

Pinner, 1972.   MARGARET E. DICKINSON.

Contents

List of Illustrations

Here, fold on fold, still lives
The richly woven chronicle
Of pleasure, passion, occupation—

Things owned in pride and love
Still keep the touch of fingers lost in dust;

Things once looked upon enclose the secrets
Of eyes which see no more.

E. M. Almedingen.

Part One

Two Men on a Horse

1

At a time when England, transformed by the civilising influence of the Norman Conquest, was about to enter the fuller and vital life of the West; when law and registration, with moral recognition of dues and rights, were taking shape under the feudal system, a knight from northern France came riding through that part of the West Saxon country known as Berkshire.

He threaded the broad unbroken stretch of forest reaching from Windsor to the near middle of the county, and so onto a chalky ridge bounding the southern side of the Thames. Here the river, overlooked by beech woods, was broader than usual, and curving away from the road behind it where clustered the village of Bustlesham.

He was riding on a royal errand. He was Henry de Ferrers, and according to Wace, the poet-priest of Bayeux, he had spurred with the Norman cavalry up the slope near Hastings in the onsets that shattered the battle-line of Harold. Now he was one of the commissioners entrusted by King William with the task of checking and recording the sources of the royal income.

The great register they made, part of the Norman passion for order, tabulation and discipline, and since called by the name of Domesday Book, was said, with pardonable exaggeration, to include the taxable value of every possession in manor or village down to the last swine. De Ferrers contented himself with saying of Bustlesham that there was a church, two slaves, twenty six acres of meadow, and some vines. The church stood at the north end of the village on the river bank, probably on the site where de Ferrers' countrymen were to lay the first stone of the present parish church in the year 1190.

The manor (a term originally restricted to a house of local importance, but later used to cover an entire estate and its tenants) had been held in Edward the Confessor's time by Bondig, called the Staller, a word that meant horse-thane or constable. After him had come Godric, sheriff of Berkshire, who had either fallen at Hastings or been dispossessed by the Conqueror for having opposed the invasion.

De Ferrers had already been well rewarded for his part in the Norman venture. His holdings numbered 220 in fourteen different counties; and in the year of the survey, 1086, he acquired the manor of Bustlesham.

Henry was succeeded by his son Robert, who was created earl by King Stephen in 1138. Robert was one of those many Normans who showed an almost equal regard for military and religious matters; and the little we know about him reflects both those, to us, widely different interests.

The northern part of the country, where English and Scot raided each other, was seldom quiet; and in the year of Robert's earldom the Scots, under their King David, crossed the border and came within reach of Northallerton, in the North Riding.

Robert gathered the men of Derbyshire, where his family was most powerful, and joined forces with one of the soldier-prelates of the time, Thurstan, Archbishop of York.

The Scots were defeated at what is known as the Battle of the Standard, a name derived from a fantastic erection that was brought on to the field to serve as rallying point and inspiration to the Norman-English army. This was a wheeled platform with a central mast from which fluttered the banners of patron saints connected with York and Durham, the mast being surmounted by the Host in a silver pyx.

The devotional side of Robert's nature was revealed when, back at Bustlesham, he decided to grant the manor to an Order whose members personified the prevailing ideal of a fighting man who was also a man of prayer.

2

The earliest form of established life recorded at the future Abbey of Bisham (to which the name of Bustlesham became abbreviated) was the outcome, like so much generated at that period, of a Gallic dream. It was, again, primarily religious, being concerned with the flow of pilgrims from many parts of Europe who braved the torments of travel by sea to worship at the Holy Places.

Those sites and shrines were then in the hands of Turks, or Saracens, who ranged far and wide along strategic points of coast-line, roadway and desert, to harass or murder the pilgrims whose only protective measure was to travel in numbers.

This state of affairs troubled the mind of Hugh de Payans, a gentleman from the province of Champagne in eastern France, who early in the 12th century decided to form a body of Christian knights to protect the travellers. Such a body could also serve to act as a more or less permanent nucleus to the Crusading armies, who at times, either through weariness or a sense of frustration, tended to abandon their original purpose of defending the Holy Places.

The monastic communities that covered Europe provided Hugh with a model for his new foundation. Their rule, embodying the usual vows of poverty, chastity and obedience, was based in general on the Rule of St. Benedict; but whereas their spirit was primarily peaceful, Hugh's fellowship was a fighting one, expert in combat and bound by military discipline as well as by vows.

Their first regular quarters were on the site of Solomon's temple in Jerusalem, and their full official title, the Poor Fellow Soldiers of Christ and the Temple of Solomon, soon became shortened to the Poor Knights of the Temple, or Knights Templars.

At their head was a Grand Master. Their leading category was formed by knights and chaplains, all of noble blood, while sergeant-commoners or servants made up a lesser or inferior degree. Their dress or uniform consisted of a white mantle marked with the blazon of an eight-pointed star, in red, worn over a tunic, and with chain mail that covered the legs. Their head-dress was of iron, as were their shoes and shoulder pieces; their arms were a sword, lance and dagger, with a large shield.

They formed what may be called the Guards Brigade of the crusading armies. No Templar went into battle expecting quarter; they gave none; and a Templar who fell or was dragged from his horse, aware of a dagger at his throat, never thought of saving his life by offering ransom or signalling a change of faith.

This military Order won the favour of St. Bernard of Clairvaux, whose voice was the most influential in Christendom. Its rule was confirmed by Pope Honorius II, and a later decree emancipated the Templars from all authority save that of the Pope.

They carried into battle, as gonfalon or standard, a banner that was parti-coloured, black as well as white; and their badge, depicting the Agnus Dei and two knights mounted on a single horse, was a reminder of the basic rules of poverty and humility. Their appearance provided a contradiction, in that their hair was cut short while their beards could straggle to any length. Some of their living conditions corresponded to those pertaining in strictly enclosed monastic Orders. They slept, in part of their clothes, in dormitories; they had no rich food or intoxicating liquors; they avoided chess, dice, theatrical performances, and the company of women; and, as a commentary on the style of the age, they were pledged not to wear pointed shoes.

The communities subordinate to the main central home of the Templars were known as preceptories, and these, with their widespread appeal to chivalry and devotion, sprang up in several parts of Europe. Hugh de Payans met Henry I of England when the latter was visiting his Norman dukedom, and as a result the Templars were soon established in parts of Essex, Lincolnshire, Hertfordshire, and Scotland.

3

The first London preceptory was in Chancery Lane, but this proved too small, and a far finer site was provided with a circular church, still standing, that was consecrated in the presence of Henry II. Its grounds lined the Thames from Whitefriars, marked by the present Carmelite Street, to Temple Bar. The Master of the English Templars sat in Parliament as the chief ecclesiastical baron of the realm.

The anarchy that ravaged much of Stephen's reign (1135–1154) scarcely affected the patronage and extension of the Church; and it was during this time that Robert de Ferrers, soon after receiving his earldom, granted the manor of Bisham to the new Order of warrior-monks. Some years later, when the Court was at Woodstock, Stephen sanctioned the deed, confirming that the manor be given to the poor Brethren of the Temple in perpetual alms, "well in peace, free and quietly," with church, wood, plain, meadows, pasture, lands and mills, that were freed from all secular exactions.

The mills referred to were some little way up stream, on the same side, where the name Temple, as applied to a hamlet, survives to this day.

In view of their discipline, and the fact that the Order experienced no reforms or branching out process, it may be safely assumed that the life of the Bisham Templars in no wise differed from that prevailing in their other foundations.

We know that at Bisham they kept three chaplains for regular services and to offer Mass for the souls of Richard I, his predecessors, and for Queen Eleanor, wife of Edward I.

Meals were accompanied by a reading from Scripture, otherwise silence prevailed and the courtesies of the table were exchanged by making sign language. There were normally three meals a day, with meat or poultry served twice a week, and wine if the Master, or the weather, so dictated. The sick could be given a dispensation to eat eggs and butter in Lent, while other invalid fare included fried slices of stag's horn in soup laced with wine, and made in three different flavours in honour of the Persons of the Trinity.

On every other weekday throughout the year the Templars observed an essential provision of religious life by giving alms to the poor of Bisham. In addition, on each 5th of March, some fifty people of the neighbourhood each received a loaf of bread, two herring, and a half-bottle of beer. A certain Adam de Char was given, for the whole of his life, threepence daily for food and ten shillings yearly to provide him with clothes.

Another instance of what was quaintly called the privilege of "sitting and eating" was the grant accorded to John de Opledon for his services, in house and garden, to the Templars. It consisted of his food "for ever," an annual outfit, and a pension of five shillings to be paid in two equal instalments at Easter and at Michaelmas. If the recipient of this or any other form of regular charity became too old or infirm to sit at table with the others, his meals were to be served in "a decent room." A yearly pension of five marks, and one bushel of corn, was paid to the vicar of Bray, near Maidenhead, where the Templars held some land.

In England, as elsewhere in the West, the kings continued to show marked favour to the Templars. Their early donations of land, churches, and worldly possessions were ratified; they were conceded the privilege of felling trees in woods they possessed, and of clearing and cultivating land, without bailiff's licence; they were declared exempt from royal and sheriffs' subsidies, and from the duty of supplying cartage, beasts of burden, or any kind of boat used for transport; they were freed from any obligation attached to the building of royal residences, from taxes on roads and bridges, and from every kind of toll in markets, fairs, or ferries throughout the kingdom.

The deed executed by Stephen was confirmed by Henry II (1154–1189) in a document that gives the name of the Bisham Master. "Know that I have given and, by this my present charter, have confirmed to Brother Osto and the Knights of the Temple, the manor of Bisham and forty acres of cultivated forest land, and the mills and fisheries of the said manor in free and perpetual alms."

There is also an agreement signed by Richard I in 1197, whereby the Templars at Bisham conveyed a hide of land to Henry FitzHenry—a hide being perhaps 120 acres, or enough land to support one household and its dependants. In return for this, the said FitzHenry relinquished a freehold in his possession that had a yearly value of six shillings and eightpence.

In the following reign of John (1199–1216) a contract was made at Westminster between the Templars at Bisham and a local landowner, Philip de Oxhey. The latter made over to the Templars one hide of land, for which the Templars paid

a yearly rent of sixteen shillings, half to be paid on the Feast
of the Assumption and the remainder at Michaelmas.

4

With the Templars established at Bisham, the overlordship
of the manor remained with the family of de Ferrers until
1266, when the name of Lancaster, which was destined to
attain a leading and ominous significance in later stages of our
history, came into prominence. An earl of that house,
Edmund, the second son of Henry III, received Bisham together with other grants formerly held by Robert de Ferrers.

Edmund was known as Crouchback, perhaps on account of
some deformity, or because of some waggish play on the
words "crossed-back;" for gossip had it that he was really the
eldest son of Henry III, but wise counsel had insisted that he
be passed over as not fit to govern.

The nickname was part of the gentle ridicule and belittling
rumour that followed Edmund despite the greatness that his
birth—he became High Steward of England, he occupied the
Savoy Palace in London, and was buried in the chapel of the
kings at Westminster Abbey—thrust upon him. He had travelled across Europe in the wake of one of the crusading
armies that by then were drifting to failure, and his reputation
was henceforth coloured by the stigma of fiasco. He was
stamped as being more truly middle class than aristocratic, by
insisting that every one of his debts must be paid before he
was buried.

His son Thomas, whose doubtful year of birth was 1277,
increased the resources of the family and added to the succession of stepping-stones that later led it to the throne. He had
five earldoms and a number of manors, including Bisham, for
which holding he paid the King a yearly rent of £46. He was a
typical representative of the barons who, from the time of
Magna Carta, kept up a constant, often disguised but determined nibbling, at the royal power until it fell apart.

It was ultimately gathered up by Lancaster's descendants;
and those who were overlords at Bisham in the 14th and 15th
centuries were to have their lives interrupted, or cut short, by
the turmoil and usurpations that were part of the process.

5

Meanwhile the fate of the Templars was being decided across the Channel.

The Crusades had ended in military failure for the West. Jerusalem had fallen to the Turks in 1244; but it was the capture of Acre, forty-seven years later, that ended the era of Christian aspiration in the Holy Land.

The Templars lived up to their high reputation, achieved in barely a century, to the last. The Grand Master and the Marshal of the Order, surrounded by enemy dead, fell in an epic defence of St. Anthony's Gate as the Turks swarmed into Acre; and Templars, acting as rearguard, were the last to confront the banners of the half-moon as the defeated Christian remnants withdrew from the mainland.

But a still greater danger awaited the Templars once they had dispersed to their preceptories all over Europe. The Order, always well patronised, had become rich and powerful; inordinately so, and to such an extent that the French King Philip IV, known as "the Fair," cast envious eyes upon their possessions. Philip was over proud and pious in practice, with a temper that was probably made worse by the hair-shirt he habitually wore; and he employed a violent propagandist (who was perhaps a lawyer) to bring about the ruin of the Templars.

Some of the charges levelled against them were frankly ridiculous. If they were guilty in any respect it may have been in the field of financial speculation, though even that cannot be proved. Suspicion was cast on their rule of secrecy, and the fact that no outsider could attend their Chapter meetings—a provision by no means unusual.

But why, it was asked, should every crack and keyhole in the room where they met be stopped up beforehand? It was surely to keep their evil and idolatrous practices from being made public. They were secret murderers and in league with the Moslems; they despised the Sacraments; their novices were required to spit upon the Cross; they worshipped a cat that was really the devil, they held homosexual orgies, and were attended by demons in female form.

Once his case was built up Philip pressed the reigning Pope,

Clement V, for a condemnation of the Templars; and Clement, a flabby-minded and unhealthy creature, gave way. On the 12th October 1307 every Templar in France was arrested. Many were burnt at the stake, still holding to the discipline of their Order and proclaiming its innocence on every count.

The campaign was then carried into every part where the Templars had been established; and it is one of the few things laid to the credit of Edward II that, for a time, he made a show of resistance on behalf of the English Templars.

He favoured the Order, and he knew Bisham—it may be noted that among the manorial papers is an indenture for the carrying of timber and planks, from Bisham to Westminster, for the making of stands and barriers at his coronation.

When the Templars were threatened he wrote to Philip the Fair, whose daughter Isabella was Edward's Queen, declaring his belief in the Order's integrity and dismissing the stories that were built up against them. He followed this up early in December by a letter to the Pope, reminding him that he should protect rather than persecute the Templars.

But before this letter could reach Rome, Edward received a directive from the Pope calling for the suppression of all Templar properties within the kingdom.

This was too much for Edward to oppose. He gave way, and on December 15th he had all members of the Order detained while their affairs were investigated. The sheriffs were required to take over "all lands, tenements, goods and chattels" of the Order, and to see that each Knight was "decently maintained" out of the confiscated property.

But Edward was still reluctant to come down heavily on the Order. The investigation dragged on for months. The Knights were held in what today would be called an open prison, from which they could wander off as they felt inclined. Only a few were brought back for interrogation, and when faced with the catalogue of their supposed crimes the only one to which they admitted was that of secrecy. They knew nothing of the Order's affairs in other countries.

6

The Pope had decreed that the confiscated estates were to

pass to the one other fighting brotherhood that had always rivalled the Templars in their proudest qualities—the Knights of St. John of Jerusalem, or Knights Hospitallers, who may still be found today as the Knights of Malta.

For some reason Bisham was not included in the transfer; but in any case Edward stood firm over this and refused to make the Thamesside preceptory over to the Church. He declared he knew how to handle the property in a way most acceptable to God; and he appears to have made good his claim that Templar lands were forfeit to the Crown, since in 1308 Robert de Hanstede was appointed, by Edward, as keeper of the manor.

This state of affairs was still pertaining in July 1309, when Richard Damory, a former sheriff of Berkshire and Oxfordshire, made an inventory of the Bisham house which was sent to the office of the Lord Treasurer Remembrancer.

Written in an atrocious mixture of dog-Latin, old French, and emerging English, it gives the following items among those found at the Bisham house when ex-Sheriff Damory and his clerk moved in. The list points to a way of living that was little short of meagre, and completely exonerates the Bisham Templars from any suspicion of extravagance.

In the *HALL*—five long tables, seven pairs of trestles, and fire-irons.

KITCHEN—a salt mill valued at two shillings, a pestle and mortar, and a "bukettum" (bucket) bound with iron.

"LARDARIO" (larder)—forty bacons, a salting tub, sixty pounds of grease worth twelve shillings and fourpence, and three meat hooks worth a shilling the lot.

CELLAR—one barrel of cider, ten empty and three broken barrels.

DAIRY—seven "bukettos" (another variation on "bucket") and two "chirnos for making butiro" (churns for butter).

BAKEHOUSE—a couple of furnaces valued at twenty shillings.

FORGE—fourteen quarters of sea coal and an "anfelt" (anvil).

GARDENER'S HOUSE—a quantity of hempseed and a rake with iron spikes, estimated value threepence.

There is also mention of a ploughshare, priced at seven-pence, and a sledge (hammer?).

The stock consisted of twenty-eight oxen, with boars and pigs (forty-nine in all), two horses, a palfrey for the preceptor, two donkeys, nine peacocks and peahens, and three swans. There were six hives of bees. The total value of goods registered was £132.12.7d.

It appears that Edward, in spite of his weakness and intransigence, was still able to hold off the claims of the Pope, since for some time subsequent to the making of the inventory the Templar house at Bisham was in the hands of Roger de Wingfield, one of the King's clerks.

During Edward II's reign part of the building was occupied by a trio of ladies. They were Elisabeth de Burgh, daughter of the Earl of Ulster; her daughter Marjorie, and Christine, the sister of Robert Bruce, the warrior-king and national hero of Scotland.

Elisabeth was Bruce's wife, and the three had been captured during the wars with Edward I. Following Bruce's defeat, they had taken refuge on the Isle of Rathlin, off the coast of Antrim. Edward had captured them and sent them south as hostages. They were held at Bisham under the custody of John de Bentley, the King's yeoman.

Whether the whole of their time in England was spent there we cannot tell; but they were not finally released until Bruce's arms triumphed over the English at Bannockburn in 1314.

In spite of the many structural alterations since carried out, it is still possible, by restricting one's view to the hall, the solar or withdrawing chamber, and kitchen, to gain some impression of the original Bisham building occupied by the Knights.

The entrance porch, with its groined vaulting, moulded ribs, and purbeck marble shafts with capitals, gives on to a door that, with its iron work, is plainly as old as the porch. The door admits to the hall with its unusually spacious measurement of more than fifty-two feet by thirty-three. It has a plain braced rafter roof, which may be original, the oak timbers being thirty-five feet long and nearly twelve inches thick. Some of these timbers, in the centre of the roof, were found, during alterations, to bear traces of smoke, an intimate relic of the 12th and 13th centuries when the place was warmed by fire on an open hearth, and the smoke went out by way of a louver in the roof.

Restoration revealed a window of the same period, with St. Peter holding a key and St. John holding a chalice, painted on either side above the three "lights."

To the west of the porch one can see arches leading to the old kitchen, the dairy, cellar, and a "lyttle woode-yard." Behind the hall gallery is the solar, with a twin-lighted window that today, as in the time of the Templars, reflects the changing colours of sun and cloud from over the Thames valley.

In assessing the overlordship and occupation of property in the Middle Ages we are faced with a complicated pattern. But by cutting through a mass of legal jargon and feudalistic terms, it can be asserted that the former preceptory was sometimes occupied by Edward II while Thomas of Lancaster held the nominal overlordship of Bisham.

Among the matters dealt with by Edward were the repair of a water mill at Bisham and the building up of the river wall at Temple, which had been damaged by floods. There was also the purchase of a boat for the use of men towing barges, plying from London, in the often difficult way upstream between Bisham and Henley. An account signed by Stephen of Abingdon, butler, is for a tun of wine delivered for the King at Bisham.

During this time the opposition, that unhinged the latter part of Edward's reign, was building up; due in part to the flaws in his own insufficient nature, and to the scheming of a baronial clique with Thomas, Earl of Lancaster, at their head.

PART TWO

Edwardian Interlude

1

Edward's particular weakness, which in a king amounted to vice (though to what extent it was sensual or ideological we cannot tell) was to elevate certain men, mostly undeserving, about him, and to heap them with favours. The most notorious of these mushroom advisers was young Piers Gaveston, a Gascon with all the verve of his race, whom Edward married to his niece, Margaret of Gloucester, and who was created Earl of Cornwall.

Gaveston carried Curtana, the Sword of Mercy, at Edward's coronation, and buckled the golden spur, emblem of knighthood and chivalry, on his sovereign's right foot. But Gaveston and the barons hated each other. He created a stir at a tournament held at Wallingford when he thundered up, at the head of 200 knights, and came near routing the assembled guests. He overthrew some of his rivals in the tilting yard. He noted their expressions, their quirks and physical failings, and flung out nicknames that reached the ears of those he ridiculed.

The Earl of Warwick was "the black hound;" my Lord of Lincoln was "burst belly," while pompous Thomas of Lancaster was reduced to being "the fiddler." Warwick's reaction was the most subdued and the most deadly. "Let him call me hound. One day the hound will bite him."

The barons waited, and so did Edward's wife. She was Isabella, a daughter of that Philip IV who persecuted the Templars. She was handsome, full of sharp purpose; perhaps one of those women with a touch of snake in their compositions. But, in fairness, she had much to contend with from the first.

She had seen her husband surrounded by persons of his own sex and receiving chorussed compliments that, more rightly, should have been hers. She had seen her wedding presents, from her father, passed over to one of them. She had been literally pensioned off, by her husband, with an allowance of twenty shillings a day. Edward carried a knife in his stocking, hoping that one day he would be able to rid himself of Isabella; and he let it be known that, if the knife failed, he was ready to crush her with his teeth.

The widespread feeling of grievance, and their own lust for power, made the barons strike. Gaveston went into exile; but after being recalled by Edward he was finally captured, on the strength of a promise that his captors treacherously broke, at Scarborough Castle.

He was hurried south, towards his own holding at Wallingford; but while resting at Deddington, near Banbury, he was roused in the middle of the night and forced to ride, the centre of a ghostly procession, through the warm June darkness made hideous by shouts and the noise of random trumpets, with torchlight over all.

At the end of the ride he found himself on enemy soil, with enemies about him. There was Warwick, the "hound" whose land it was, and Lancaster "the fiddler;" and now, emptied of pride and no longer the upstart, Gaveston flung himself on the ground before Lancaster, clutching his feet and begging for pity from "his gentle lord."

But there was no pity or gentleness in the little procession that formed again and conducted the prisoner to Blacklow Hill, a mile or two north of Warwick, where the head that had been rendered giddy by royal favour rolled on the blood-stained turf. Gaveston's body was placed on a ladder and carried to Oxford by four men who were described as cobblers.

With Gaveston gone, Edward consoled himself by patronising Hugh Despenser, a favourite who was also a gentleman, though no less offensive to the baronial party on that score. Despenser's father, another Hugh, came in for some of the lavish pickings that fell to his son.

Between them they amassed a considerable fortune; and

once again the barons, led by Lancaster, rose against the King and his circle of friends. At first they succeeded in getting the Despensers banished, a step, according to the barons, that redounded "to the honour of God and Holy Church."

But in 1322 the Despensers returned, and the King, bent on restoring them, took up arms against the rebels. Lancaster (who had been treating with the Scots under the inappropriate pseudonym of "King Arthur") struck north, and in a clash at Boroughbridge, Yorkshire, the barons were beaten.

Their leader was taken to Pontefract, placed on a pony without a bridle, as a sign of indignity, and hurried to execution. His last prayer held a germ of reproach that, considering his sustained opposition to Edward, was not without humour: "Have mercy on me, King of Heaven, for my earthly King has forsaken me."

It was commonly believed that Lancaster (whose death ended, for the time being, the Lancastrian connection with Bisham) was a saint. Miracles were claimed at his tomb, and crowds flocked to kneel at his effigy which was set up in St. Paul's.

The Despensers, father and son, were now supreme. The elder became Edward's chamberlain; their territorial gifts included the county of Glamorgan; and within a few days of Lancaster's death the younger Hugh was presented with the manor of Bisham.

The custodian of the place about that time, appointed by Despenser, was Drogo Barentyn, and he was followed by William Langford. There is evidence to show that Edward and his Court visited the favourite at Bisham for the first ten days of June in 1325.

While these events were under way the Queen had gone to France, ostensibly to settle some business with her brother, now reigning as Charles IV, but in reality to rid herself of the sight of her husband and his coterie of male companions—a spectacle intolerable to most women, but especially to one who was called the "she-wolf of France."

There she became the mistress of Roger Mortimer, who had had to leave England, after a dramatic escape from the Tower, for working against Edward. They lived openly together—an act of defiance which the medieval conscience

found as shocking as the Despenser tyranny was hateful; together they formed an army that landed on the Suffolk coast,
and without attempting to encounter it Edward and the two
Despensers fled to Wales.

Very few joined them. The King was reduced to hiding in
the countryside, a common fugitive, but within a few days he
and both Despensers were taken prisoner.

Hugh the Elder was executed at Bristol. The Younger, declared robber and outlaw, and dressed in a black gown with a
wreath of nettles on his head, was hanged on a gallows fifty
feet high at Hereford. Edward was deposed and held captive
in Berkeley Castle in Gloucestershire.

"He must," the she-wolf urged upon his gaolers, "be treated severely;" and they obeyed her with such exactness that
before the end of the year, 1327, Edward was done to death.
There were no marks of violence upon his body; but his face,
formerly well chiselled and sensitive, was horribly twisted.

The manor of Bisham again reverted to the Crown. The late
King's heir, another Edward, being only fifteen, was completely overlooked or treated as a puppet by the pair who exer-
cised authority and indulged in no little state—one of their
conceits was the holding of a Round Table tournament at
Bedford.

But within three years young Edward was virtually a man;
married to Philippa of Hainault, and the father of the future
Black Prince. He was also the close friend of William Montacute, descended from a Drogo de Montacute who had stepped
ashore with the Conqueror at Pevensey and who had settled
his family in Somerset.

This William, a little older than Edward, was one of those
"handymen" who prove useful to royalty in various ways. He
fought with Edward against the Scots; he negotiated a marriage between Edward's sister and a French prince; he went
on embassy to the Papal Court at Avignon; and when Edward
needed money it was Montacute who arranged a loan of 2,000
marks.

Before long Edward resolved to assert his rightful authority
and to end the seizure of power by his mother and her para-
mour. It was known that Montacute was Edward's right-hand
man in this, and Mortimer, hearing some rumour of their

intention and trying to feel that he really stood in the shoes of a king, denounced Montacute as a traitor.

But neither Mortimer nor Isabella took the threat very seriously, and when, in October 1330, the Parliament met at Nottingham, they occupied adjoining rooms in the castle.

Montacute conferred with the governor who showed him a secret underground passage (now known as "Mortimer's hole") that led to the central apartments. Edward's party moved in at night. Led by Montacute, they broke down the door of Mortimer's chamber. Some of his followers resisted. Mortimer accounted for one of the attackers, but two of his own men were killed and Montacute finally seized and disarmed him. At the height of the struggle Isabella burst in and appealed to Edward: "Sweet son, have pity on the gentle Mortimer!"

From that hour Edward was firmly in the saddle. Mortimer was conveyed from the Tower to Tyburn Elms where he was hanged and quartered as a traitor. The Queen-mother lived for another thirty years in a state of relaxed captivity at a number of royal residences, including Windsor, Berkhamstead, Norwich, and Castle Rising in Norfolk. It appears that for a time, after Mortimer's death, Edward granted her certain revenues or privileges connected with Bisham.

PART THREE

King and Montacute

1

Edward rewarded Montacute with several of Mortimer's holdings in Kent, Hampshire, Dorsetshire, and Wales. With these went a yearly payment of 1,000 marks. He was also promised the manor of Bisham, but for some reason this was granted to Ebulo L'Estrange ("our beloved and trusted Ebulo") on condition that it passed to Montacute on Ebulo's death.

Nothing is known about Ebulo except that he was lame and a squire, and that he was accused of adultery with Countess Alice, the wife of a former Bisham overlord, Thomas of Lancaster. Ebulo married her when the execution of Thomas, after the fight at Boroughbridge, left her a widow.

Early in his reign Edward granted to his watchman, John de Hardyng (a name always to be found in the records of Bisham, and persisting to this day) thirty acres of land, one acre of meadow, and three and a half acres of woodland, the whole worth 21s. yearly, for his long service.

The close friendship between Edward III and Montacute went on without any of the jealous striving for power that marred so many loyalties in the Middle and later ages. England and France were on the threshold of the Hundred Years' War, to decide the genealogical or dynastic claims of the English monarch to the French crown; and the two men, disguised as merchants, crossed the Channel together on a mission that remains as secret to us as it was to the French.

They went north on one of the innumerable expeditions

against the Scots, and stood together at Halidon Hill where the English bowmen launched the "storm of arrows" that was soon to make them invincible. Montacute lost an eye in the campaign.

The Berkshire manor passed to him at Michaelmas, 1335, when Ebulo L'Estrange died while taking part in yet another of Edward's efforts to amalgamate the Scottish crown with his own; and two years later Montacute was created the first Earl of Salisbury.

As such he was perhaps the earliest of its lords to show a decided preference for the "mansion house" at Bisham; and that preference was continued, by others of his line, for as long as it lasted.

2

It had long been common for landowners to show their attachment to some particular saint, or religious Order, by founding a monastery or convent. The greater religious houses everywhere were established under the patronage, and the Rule, of St. Benedict. A somewhat different influence was generated by the friars, Franciscan and Dominican, in the mid-13th century; but between those epochs another way of religious life, associated with St. Augustine, entered into Europe.

This Augustine was not, of course, the apostle of the English, but the Bishop of Hippo, theologian, philosopher, and author of the *Confessions*. He promulgated no definite code of religious life, after the manner of St. Benedict; but certain of his teachings, coupled with a letter he wrote for the guidance of women living in community, came to be known as the Rule of St. Augustine, and it was soon accepted as part of a stricter system for the direction of canons serving various cathedrals.

Those of the canons who wished to follow a more regular way of life than that of the secular priesthood were formed, towards the end of the 11th century, into the Canons Regular of St. Augustine. They became popular in England, and in the 13th century numbered some 170 houses, including King Harold's favourite foundation at Waltham, Essex, and what was to be the poet Byron's birthplace, Newstead Abbey, in Nottinghamshire.

They wore a black cloak over a white rochet—a linen garment resembling a surplice with tight sleeves, and trimmed with lace—and so were known as Black, or Austin, Canons. While undertaking the normal sacerdotal and parochial work of priests, their existence was more disciplined and monastic than that of the itinerant friars, and had its own system of common prayer, fasting and silence.

A priory of this Order was established by Salisbury, under licence granted by Edward III, in close proximity to, but separate from, the mansion at Bisham. Edward laid the first stone, and the seal of its foundation was a pointed oval on which was depicted the coronation of the Virgin under a double-arched canopy. It is probable that the priory (for such was its proper title) and its church, were adapted from, or included some part, of the original Templar buildings. Among the sacred mementoes on the church altar was a silver phial containing relics of Saints Cosmas and Damian, Arabian brothers and both doctors, who were martyred early in the fourth century.

The priory underwent three changes of title. Its first dedication was to Our Lord Jesus Christ and the Blessed Virgin His Mother; a later charter referred to the Virgin Mary only; while under Richard II it was known as the Conventual Church of the Holy Trinity. The Bisham canons had a special charge to pray for the souls of the Montacute family.

The first prior, appointed in 1337, was Thomas Wiltshire. His lodgings, built of brick and timber, tile covered, and with a garden plot, stood between the river and the present Abbey. The names of some of the later priors have come down to us —Adam, prior from 1409 to (perhaps) 1422; Edward, 1423 to 1432; John, 1444; Hugh, 1446 to 1450; John, 1451 to 1455; Henry, 1469 to 1483; and William, 1492 to 1506.

The priory should have prospered. It existed under the eye of one of the most powerful men in England. Pope Benedict IX, and after him Innocent VII, appropriated the revenues of several other churches for its benefit. But the little that we know of its early record makes depressing reading. Perhaps Prior Wiltshire, and those who succeeded him, were not able governors. Perhaps they were extravagant—at one stage the average number of lay brothers and servants at Bisham was about thirty.

At any rate, an early letter refers to the priory being weighed down with debt, and complains that part of the church was for some time unfinished. The cattle, sheep and horses, were smitten with disease; the lands and crops were often ruined by floods. The actual situation did not help matters. It was not far from Reading or from Windsor, which meant that many visitors to those places applied at the priory for food and lodgment.

It was also near a highway, and the canons were expected to provide hospitality for people travelling to market; while a "pestilence," which may have been connected with the Black Death, was responsible for a falling off in rents. We do not know to what extent the plague, that in 1348 and 1349 wiped out half of the country's population, ravaged Berkshire; but with the Thames flowing through the county the barges and their cargoes were ready carriers of infection.

However, the regular revenues of the priory, or the bounty of the Salisburys, had substantially increased early in the 16th century, when the income of the place was equal to that of many larger houses.

3

With the start of the Hundred Years' War in 1337, Salisbury left Bisham and accompanied Edward across the Channel. Before long Edward was called back to England, and Salisbury took command of the army.

His headquarters were at Ypres, a name made famous nearly six centuries later as becoming the graveyard of our 1914 expeditionary force; and while there Salisbury was captured, during a raid or an ambush, and taken to Paris. For a time his life was in danger, but powerful voices were raised on his behalf and he was eventually freed on condition that he never more fought against France.

While Salisbury was being held captive a colourful incident is said to have occurred in which the central figure was his wife, Catherine, a daughter of Lord William Grandison. She too left Bisham and journeyed north to join her brother-in-law, Sir Edward Montacute, who was repelling another invasion by the Scots.

For a time the English were besieged in Wark Castle, Northumberland, and while there the presence of the Countess so "comforted" the garrison that she made every one man perform the services of two.

The Scots retreated when Edward III, who by then was back in England, marched up from York. The Countess herself opened the gates of Wark Castle to Edward. She had decked herself for the occasion, and the sudden sight of her beauty swept Edward off his feet, or, in the words of the chronicle, struck him to the heart "with a sparkle of fine love."

They entered the castle hand-in-hand. At a ball that was part of the festivities the Countess dropped her garter. Edward recovered it from among the feet of the dancers. A courtier who, like everyone present, had noted how the King's eyes seldom left Catherine, made a jesting, perhaps a half gallant, half suggestive remark. But Edward took command of the situation, and bound the garter to his own knee with the celebrated words, *Honi soit qui mal y pense*.

It has long been customary for moderns, with their anti-chivalric tendencies, to rush in and dismiss the story as a piece of romantic fiction. Certain it is that there is no reason for regarding Catherine as a ravishing beauty. There are some grounds for thinking that she has been confused with Joan, "the fair maid of Kent," a daughter of Earl Edmund.

Joan was sometime betrothed to William, the second Earl of Salisbury, but the contract was annulled and they never married. She was younger than Catherine, and obviously ornamental enough to be called the fair maid of a fair county. If the lady was Joan, the garter incident occurred at a ball held in Calais. She was twice married, her second husband being the Black Prince.

But so called legend serves a purpose in history as well as in imagination; and when Edward, in 1349, established the highest Order of English knighthood, the Garter, its motto became the words by which a love-sick King, quick to preserve the honour of a lady from blemish, turned the edge of a laughing remark.

The first Earl of Salisbury died in 1344 after taking part in a tournament at Windsor. His death is described, in what is probably an understatement, as having been caused by bruises. He was buried in the priory church (not to be confused with the parish church) at Bisham; and six years later a solemn company clad in black hoods and plumes escorted the body of his wife to what became the family burial place.

4

The second Earl of Salisbury, another William, born in 1328, resembled his father in that he was close to the person of the monarch he served—at first Edward III and after him Richard II. He held a variety of posts that illustrated his many-sided talents in military, naval and administrative matters; and at the close of his life his thoughts reverted to the riverside mansion and priory church that seemed remote from the changes and turmoil of a time that reflected the end of the Middle Ages.

He was one of the first to be honoured as Knight of the Garter; he was made Admiral of the King's Fleet, a command that extended from the mouth of the Thames westward; he was governor of the Isle of Wight, and, like most of his caste, he fought in Scotland and later in France, where he became Constable of the Army.

The Hundred Years' War was then in its early stages; and as a young man of eighteen he rode with Edward III and the small English army that hastened, for it was driven by danger, from the coast of Normandy and across the Somme valley, through the forest of Crécy and so to the little town of that name, to where a mound on a ridge today marks the site of the windmill that was the King's post during the battle.

He saw the enemy host drawn up black against the sun that broke through storm clouds, and the shattering of the French feudal cavalry under the showers of arrows that followed the summer rain. Lined up with Salisbury, and also on foot, as demanded by the English position, which was purely defensive, stood another young man of almost similar age, the Black Prince.

Ten years later Salisbury held a command in the army of

the Prince at Poitiers. Salisbury's force, although officially detailed to act as rearguard, had already made contact with the French when the Prince charged, under the folds of his great banner on which were pictured the disputed Gallic lilies, and brought back the French king as prisoner.

The attachment of the Salisburys to the ruling house led to their unqualified support of Richard II at a time when self-seeking was sapping away the ties of traditional loyalty.

The second Earl assisted at Richard's coronation in 1377; and he was close to the young King's person when there were outbreaks of lawlessness and violence in several counties following the levy of a poll tax three years later.

The peasant had, of course, hitherto been taxed, but payment had always been in labour and in dues for his land. This latest tax, however, as part of the post-feudal impact on society, brought home a realisation that money was now being demanded by a new power, the State; and popular leaders were quick to condemn the innovation as a rank injustice.

There were risings in East Anglia and the Home Counties by mobs whose anger was directed against wealthy churchmen and lawyers. London was threatened; the Archbishop of Canterbury was murdered; and on June 15th the young King Richard, accompanied by Salisbury, rode out from the Tower and confronted the rebels at Smithfield.

Salisbury, aware that Richard was possessed of a true Plantagenet spirit, urged him to temper his words with caution and gentleness. He was close to the King when the two factions met, and Richard for the first time addressed his people: "What need ye, my Masters? I will be your king. Follow me!" He saw the mayor, and after him one of the King's esquires, draw their daggers and strike the rebel leader, Wat Tyler, from his horse.

The people dispersed. They were promised charters to gratify their demands; charters that were afterwards treacherously repealed by the rising power of the Commons.

Salisbury's brother, Sir John Montacute, who had also been at Crécy, became steward to the household of Richard II. It was his son, also named John, who became the third Earl. It was therefore part of his heritage to share the family's allegiance to the Plantagenet throne that was soon to be seized by

Original porch and door of the Knights
Templars building

Knights Templars doorway with solar on
left and dormitories on right

The Templars great hall showing part
of the Bisham tapestry

The Thames at Bisham showing the church
and the Abbey beyond: from a painting by
Alfred de Bréansky

Aerial view of Abbey

Fireplace in the Great Hall, with stonework
of the Hoby period and overmantel presented by James I

The council chamber, circa 14th century,
with 18th century wall-paper

Attics above the council chamber

a descendant of the house of Thomas, Earl of Lancaster, who had held Bisham.

The life of the second Salisbury was overshadowed by a family tragedy, since he had the misfortune to cause the death of his son while jousting. The Earl ordered a brass commemorating his son to be placed in churches wherever he held lands. There must have been one at Bisham, lost at the Dissolution; but one can still be seen in All Saints' church, Calbourne, in the Isle of Wight.

Meanwhile happenings of a more peaceful nature were taking place within the compass of the priory and the mansion by the river.

In the summer of 1385 a cry of "Miracle!" was being raised in the village, and pilgrims from miles around were frequenting a spring of water that rose from beneath a chalky hill in a field that for some time took on the name of Holy-well. The site, now being disfigured by the making of a road, is on the left at the foot of Bisham hill, coming from Maidenhead.

The water was said to possess healing qualities. It cured afflictions of the eye and restored failing sight. Moreover, a bird had nested in a tree overlooking the spring, and the bird was so tame that people could handle it without a wing being fluttered.

Such marvels have never been left unexploited, and before long a self-appointed hermit moved in and shared the tree with the bird. Offerings from those who made use of the water were placed in the nest. But while the hermit profited, the church box suffered accordingly; and the affair reached the ears of the Bishop of Salisbury, Ralph Erghum, whose diocese then took in the county of Berkshire, and who was occupying a diocesan manor house at Sonning.

The Bishop decided that the veneration and the offerings made at the spring were due to the deceptions of the devil. The cures that were claimed could be attributed to the natural effect of cold water upon blear eyes—thus suggesting that such a treatment had not been previously applied. He carried his complaint to the Bishop of Lincoln, since pilgrims were coming from Marlow and other places in Buckinghamshire, a county that was then included under the Lincoln diocese.

Bishop Erghum repeated that the pilgrims were being vic-
timised by "the fancy of devilish art," by "the crooked ser-
pent," and that the happenings at the spring were a baneful
example, a detriment to the Catholic faith, and a scandal to
Holy Mother Church.

With the consent of the owner of the field, Bishop Erghum
cut down the tree with the nest and filled up the spring with
stones. But in spite of being threatened with excommunica-
tion, some "sons of the devil" from Marlow and High
Wycombe removed the obstruction and set the stream in
motion again. Bishop Erghum requested his brother of Lincoln to exercise his authority and to lead back the sheep who
had wandered from the path of the True Faith.

It is likely that the spring soon lost its significance. The
canons at the priory were doubtless concerned, while the Earl
of Salisbury could not have been remote from the affair. But
his nephew, John, who shared many of the grievances against
the Church that were being put forward in pamphlets by the
unorthodox John Wycliffe, probably smiled at yet another
instance of superstition.

Local belief in the healing properties of the spring, however,
lingered on in the minds of those who, traditionally and by
birth, were part of the district. Less than a lifetime ago there
were people still living who claimed that application of the
water (which broadens into a stream running at the base of
Quarry Woods) had removed some complaint of the eyes or
bettered their vision. In 1905 the water, after being analysed,
was said to owe any curative effect to suspended gases.

An incident of a somewhat different kind occurred when a
family gathering took place at the Bisham house of the Salisburys. One of their number was going abroad, not, as commonly stated, on a crusade (such ventures had come to an
end) but possibly to one of the more distant shrines. Among
the guests was his daughter, who was a nun at the Benedictine
convent of De Fontinbras, at Minchin or Little Marlow.

Also present was a young squire. They had known each
other well before she withdrew from the world; and now, in
spite of her veil and the assembled company, they managed to
exchange more than a few words and glances, and arranged to
make off together that very night.

When darkness fell they met on the river bank, boarded a boat, and started downstream towards Marlow. Their flight was soon noticed, and the pursuers found the couple in difficulties; for the river then was sufficiently wide-spreading to form a number of veritable lagoons that were dotted with small islands, and neither the squire, trained as he was to domestic chivalry, nor the young nun, knew how to navigate a boat through dark and winding waters.

The girl went back to her convent, and the squire, pending judgment (for persuading a nun to break her vows and elope was a weighty offence) was shut up in the turret that dominated the house before the erection of the present tower. He was so bent on escape that he tore up much of his clothing and used it as a rope to help his descent. But it broke before he reached the ground, and being badly injured he was taken into the priory.

There he was in contact with the Austin Canons, and while recovering his thoughts led him to experience a kind of reconversion. Without leaving the spot where his last worldly escapade had failed he entered the Order, and finally became the prior of the Bisham house. So it was that with the passing of the years the river, flowing downstream, from the canon in his stall to the nun in her cell, provided a bond of silent communion between the one-time lovers.

The second Earl of Salisbury, in his will, left 500 marks to embellish or complete the building of the priory church, where he marked the grave of his parents with a more imposing tomb than the original, and prepared one for himself. He was buried there in 1397.

5

There were aspects in the nature of his nephew, John, who succeeded to the earldom, that set him apart from others of his line. His adherence to Richard II, for instance, did not rest solely on his regard for a legitimate title. For he shared, with Richard, a love of the French culture that the King so typically represented. He wrote passable songs, ballads, and rondels. But he differed fundamentally from most of his kind by sympathising with the Lollards.

Lollard was a cant term for those who were rejecting the claims of religious authority in favour of individual judgment. That, as seen by people of the time, was tantamount to denying the moral basis of society; and this seeming encouragement to lawlessness was in no wise counteracted by the hymns and psalms that were an essential part of Lollard worship.

The spirit of the sect was anti-clerical; and by supporting it Salisbury became the subject of gossip that made him unpopular. He employed a Lollard chaplain, and the chapel of a property he possessed at Shenley, in Hertfordshire, was said to be a centre of profanation, where religious images were broken and the Host was held up to ridicule.

But he was firmly entrenched in Richard's favour. He was made Marshal of England, and as such he was privy to the moves to meet the threat that was being posed by Henry, Duke of Lancaster.

Henry was Richard's cousin. Always a potential danger (though his strongest claim to the throne was that he had descended from Henry III), he had been banished. But in July, 1399, he landed at Ravenspur, in the mouth of the Humber, declaring that his only purpose was to recover the lands he had forfeited on being sentenced.

Richard and his supporters, including Salisbury, fell back on Wales, which was generally regarded as the King's most promising recruiting ground. But the response was slow and disappointing. The forces gathered in the north of the country soon melted away, and Shakespeare in *Richard II* put the following words into Salisbury's mouth when the King belatedly arrived:

"One day too late, I fear me, noble lord,
Hath clouded all thy happy days on earth.
O! call back yesterday, bid time return,
And thou shalt have twelve thousand fighting men."

Richard, almost entirely abandoned, surrendered on condition that he kept his crown. Henry agreed, but promptly proceeded to break his promise. Having secured Richard's deposition he was made King within three months of having landed. Richard was committed to Pontefract Castle, where, early in the new year, he was murdered, perhaps by being starved. Salisbury spent some time in the Tower, and on being released he was soon plotting to overthrow the man who had been proclaimed Henry IV.

Shortly before Christmas the conspirators met at Abbot's House, Westminster. Besides Salisbury, several earls were involved in the plot which included the Duke of Surrey, Richard's brother. It was arranged to seize Henry on 12th Day, the Feast of the Epiphany, when he attended the jousts at Windsor. But Henry got wind of the affair, and the conspirators scattered.

Salisbury and the Duke of Surrey made for the west, still hoping to gather men in that part of the country. But they were followed and nearly cut off. There was a sharp fight at Maidenhead bridge, from which Surrey and Salisbury managed to disengage when the January darkness fell. They continued as far as Cirencester, where the two leaders, too exhausted to set a proper guard at the gates, took lodgings at an inn.

News of their intended design must have followed them; for the mayor, described as "a man of sense and courage," roused the town. The inn was attacked, and just as the spirited defence put up by Surrey and Salisbury was on the point of failing, one of Salisbury's men set fire to a nearby building.

In the diversion thus effected the fugitives escaped and sought shelter in the abbey. But the mob, more intent on demonstrating loyalty to the new King than on regarding the right of sanctuary, broke in; and after some form of rough justice or hurried trial, Salisbury was beheaded. He was buried at Cirencester, while his head was sent to be spiked with those of other declared traitors on London Bridge.

Some years later his widow, Maud, petitioned the reigning Henry V for permission to move her husband's body. This was granted; and so the remains of John, third Earl of Salisbury were transferred to Bisham.

6

Thomas, the fourth Earl of Salisbury, born in 1388 and therefore only twelve when his father was beheaded, became the most noted of his line. He served under three Henrys, the

IV, V, VI, and mostly in France, where the Hundred Years' War was mounting to a climax.

As the most successful English commander, "the mirror of all martial men," his titles included Lieutenant-General of Normandy, and, under the Duke of Bedford's Regency, the Vice-Regent and Lieutenant of the King in France. The earldom his father had forfeited for opposing Henry IV was restored to him in 1421.

His personal retinue, part of the force that crossed the Channel with Henry V, and for which he was paid at the rate of twelve pence a day, consisted of three knights, thirty-six esquires, forty men-at-arms, and eighty mounted archers.

He was present at Harfleur (converted by soldier slang into "Harefleet") and he rode with Henry into the town when it capitulated after a siege of five weeks. He was with the King at Agincourt, on the dreary October night preceding St Crispin's Day, when the moon was lost behind clouds and the only illumination came from enemy camp fires—within their glow the confident French threw dice for the captives they would take on the morrow; and he was one of Shakespeare's band of brothers,

"Harry the King, Bedford and Exeter,
Warwick and Talbot, Salisbury and Gloucester . . . "

who took their places on the rain-sodden soil (his men kissed it, to show their allegiance to Almighty God and St. George), to meet and overcome the onsets of the Dauphin's chivalry.

The campaign marked a series of triumphs for Salisbury. He conducted sieges and captured town after town. One of the places he invested, further north, was Mons, where the cathedral of St. Waudru, that looked down on our 1914 army, was in process of being planned. He took the castle of Orsay, and led those of its garrison who survived, bareheaded and with ropes about their necks, into Paris. The town of Verneuil in the hilly country of the Perche, surrendered to him on conditions that Salisbury promised to observe. Certain of his followers resented this, and were on the point of violating his pledge when Salisbury slew the leaders of those who murmured with his own hands.

A pivot of the campaign of 1428 was the siege of

Orleans, the gate to the south; and in the autumn of that year Salisbury moved down to capture it.

Throughout October he was driving the French back from their forward positions and softening up the outer defences. On the 27th he stood with his esquire, Sir Thomas Gargrave, at a window overlooking the progress of the siege; while in the beleaguered city the gunner's son, a mere lad, decided to take a chance shot at the encircling English.

The missile fired was a heavy ball that crashed through the iron work of the window and into the stone wall of the place where the watchers were standing. Gargrave was killed at once, while part of Salisbury's face, including an eye, was carried away. He was taken to Meung, on the Loire, where he died a week later, exhorting those about him, with his last breath, not to give up the siege.

But the resolution with which his captains sought to sustain it counted for little, since before many months were out the future St. Joan of Arc rode into the town, in full armour and under the folds of her lilied banner, and shattered the English siege line.

Salisbury's first wife had been Eleanor, a daughter of Thomas, Earl of Kent. She died early and Salisbury married again, this time Alice, daughter of Thomas Chaucer, a knight of Ewelme in Oxfordshire, and grand-daughter of Geoffrey Chaucer the poet.

After Salisbury's death she married William de la Pole, Earl of Suffolk, who met his end in a way that illustrates the anarchy that was leading to the Wars of the Roses.

After being impeached in 1450, Suffolk was crossing the Channel to enter upon a period of exile imposed, as a friendly gesture, by Henry VI, who wished to save Suffolk's life. But on the way Suffolk was arrested, by one of the King's ships, and after six blows, delivered by a rusty sword, his head was severed. The second part of Shakespeare's *Henry VI* gives a false impression of the episode.

Salisbury, in his will, left instructions for a chantry, in honour of the Blessed Virgin, to be erected in the priory church at Bisham. He also planned a tomb for himself and his two wives. This was to be four feet high and to consist of three divisions for as many bodies. The centre place, higher than those on either side by two feet six inches, was for himself. One of the remaining places was for Eleanor, his first wife, while the remaining division was for the Lady Alice, in respect of whom Salisbury added, as though with a tentative after-thought, "if she will." The tomb was to be of marble, with portraits and epitaphs in brass.

But the Lady Alice, who survived Salisbury, did not will to join him. She chose instead to take her rest in the parish church at Ewelme; and when the English general, with part of his face muffled, was laid in the centre of the tomb at Bisham, one side of the monument he had planned was left vacant.

PART FOUR

The Shadow of the Roses

1

The latter part of the reign of Henry VI (he was murdered in 1471) brought a change in the manorial line at Bisham, together with more profound upheavals in the political and national structures that governed it.

The local change was affected by the marriage of Alice, daughter of the fourth Earl of Salisbury, who left no son, to Richard Neville. His father was Ralph, Earl of Westmorland and the Earl Marshal of England. The Nevilles were a family of the first importance. One of their name had commanded the fleet that in September, 1066, carried Duke William's host from the shores of Normandy to Pevensey Bay.

They had since increased as a territorial, military, and financial power, not far removed from the throne. Richard Neville, who was already Knight of the Garter, Warden of the Marches, and Governor of Carlisle, now claimed, in right of his wife, the title of Earl of Salisbury, a claim that was confirmed by Henry VI; and this alliance between Richard and Alice meant that the Bisham estate now descended, through the female line, from the Montacutes to the Neville and Warwick families.

The Warwick title came into the story when Richard's son, of the same name and the future King-maker, was created Earl of Warwick in 1449. A younger son of Richard, John, became the Marquess of Montagu and Earl of Northumberland.

The resources and organising power of the Nevilles and

similar families were called into action when civil war resulted from the claims to the throne, put forward by rival factions, during the chequered lifetime of Henry VI.

Henry had no better right to inheritance than that he was the grandson of the Lancastrian Henry IV. Opposed to this was the claim of Richard, Duke of York, who, according to the usage of the time, was legitimate heir-presumptive to the throne in that he was Plantagenet and could boast of a double descent from Edward III.

Richard's right gained a further practical stimulus from the fact that Henry was feeble-minded, partly imbecile; and during one of his serious breakdowns, when he could scarcely speak and recognised no one, Richard was appointed Protector of the Realm.

With Henry's partial recovery, and York's removal from office, the rival houses gathered strength and the Wars of the Roses began. The Nevilles lined up with their Yorkist connections; and on May 22nd, 1455, shouts of "A Warwick! A Warwick!" were heard as war-cry in the streets of St. Albans where the sides clashed for the first time. The feeble Henry was there defeated and captured.

The struggle continued in an atmosphere of general confusion, contradiction, and changing loyalties. Salisbury won a victory at Blore Heath, in Staffordshire. But next the Lancastrians triumphed, and York and Warwick fled overseas. They returned, and in July, 1460, after a battle outside Northampton, Henry was again captured and taken to London by Warwick.

But Henry's wife, Margaret of Anjou, a niece of the French King Charles VII, and a woman of military mettle who, unusual for her kind, was as handsome as she was vigorous, was concentrating forces in the north.

An army under the Earl of Salisbury and Richard of York marched to encounter her, and was totally defeated at Wakefield. The Duke of York and Salisbury's son, Thomas, were killed.

Salisbury, though wounded, was taken to Pontefract. No time was wasted by the Lancastrian Lord Clifford, "the butcher," in sending him to the block, after which his head, together with that of Richard, was put above one of the York gates.

Alice, Countess of Salisbury, died at Bisham of grief when she heard the news; and it reached her quickly. The battle fought on December 30th, 1460, was known of in London, 182 miles distant, on January 2nd 1461. With Salisbury's death his Bisham estate passed to the King-maker.

The fight against Lancaster was carried on by York's son, Edward, with Warwick still in the forefront of affairs. In March, 1461, he led a strong force that came to grips with Margaret's army at Towton, not far from York. When the armies sighted each other Warwick, who knew the value of drama, stabbed his horse to show his followers that, come what may, he had lost his chance of flying from the field.

It was Palm Sunday, and the battle took place in a blizzard. Warwick's victory was so complete that, with the success of his party seemingly assured, Edward was crowned, the fourth King of that name. He was still a minor, and for the next three years Warwick took over the direction of affairs. Apart from acting in the King's name he was Lord Great Chamberlain of England, Lord High Steward, Warden of the East Marches on the Border, and caretaker of Dover Castle. "There was none in England," it was said, "of the half possessions that he had."

2

While he was still being acclaimed as the victor of Towton, Warwick took part in a three-fold funeral ceremony at Bisham.

The remains of Salisbury, Warwick's father, who was executed at Pontefract, and of Thomas his son, who had fallen at Wakefield, were removed from their Yorkshire graves and brought south for burial at Bisham. A procession was formed about a mile from Marlow, where their coffins, together with a third coffin that held the body of Salisbury's wife, were placed in a chariot, or hearse, that was decked with the arms and bannerols of St. George. The six horses drawing the chariot were preceded by two conductors, dressed in black, two Kings of Arms, and two heralds.

Then came the dead Earl's son and heir, Warwick the King-maker, an impressive figure with more than a touch of popular glory about him, riding at the head of sixteen knights. Waiting to meet them at the priory church was the Bishop of Exeter, Lord Chancellor; the Bishop of Salisbury and the Bishop of St. Asaph; Lord Hastings, Chamberlain; the Duke of Clarence and the Duke of Suffolk; the Earl of Worcester; Lord Fitzhugh; their ladies, and a company of heralds and pursuivants.

The ceremony lasted into the following day that opened with High Mass. After the Gospel the two Kings of Arms went to the west door where they admitted a mounted man-at-arms who, still riding and bearing an axe ("the point downward being in the Arms of the Earl") went to the choir door. There he dismounted and stood, holding his horse, to receive the offerings of the mourners.

The Earl of Warwick, escorted by knights and heralds, offered the Mass penny. Then the barons, attended by heralds, crossed to the choir-door where the man-at-arms delivered up his horse. The offerings made by the principal guests varied, according to rule, from a groat to twenty-two pence. The man-at-arms offered a noble (about six and eight-pence). After the delivery of the Crest of Arms, with the shield, sword and helm, the lords made a presentation offering of cloth-of-gold. The ceremony closed with the Kings of Arms and the heralds placing the dead Earl's shield and helm at the head of his coffin, with the sword on the right side and the standard at his feet.

The Kings of Arms received £4.10.0 in funeral fees for each of the two days; the heralds were paid forty-five shillings, and the pursuivants twenty shillings and sixpence.

3

In his capacity as the virtual ruler, Warwick had his own plans for Edward, aimed at securing the future of the young King and himself. But Edward's development kept pace with a growing desire to escape from Warwick's leading-strings, and when he was twenty-two he contracted a secret marriage with Elizabeth Woodville.

She was a widow, connected with the smaller Lancastrian gentry; and by bringing her family into the focus of royalty, Edward antagonised many of his strongest supporters.

The cry was heard, "Warwick to save England!" And the King-maker proceeded to justify the trust reposed in him by leading a revolt against Edward, who fled abroad. Warwick filled the gap by restoring the dazed Henry, which meant, of course, that Warwick resumed the place of power he had held during Edward's minority. But this sudden change of loyalty did not serve him for long.

Edward landed in the Humber, and was soon at the head of an army that met Warwick's forces at Hadley Green, a half-mile from Barnet. It was April the 14th, 1471; Easter Sunday. A thick mist enveloped the armies. Warwick relinquished the privilege of a leader and fought on foot. There can be no clear reading of the battle, where flanks were turned, lines over-lapped, and men could scarcely make out the badges on the banners that should have guided them.

But Warwick's men broke; he left the main struggle and, helped by the covering mist, went in search of his horse. But he was surrounded on the way and cut down. His brother John, Marquess of Montagu, was also killed.

Their battered bodies were exposed for two days, "open and naked," in St. Paul's, as Edward wished to demonstrate to the people that the man who had opposed him at the last, a good soldier, tireless and resourceful, but of suspect faith, was indeed dead; and when the grim spectacle had satisfied the gaping Londoners, the earthly relics of the man who had elevated or dashed down kings, together with those of his brother, were buried at Bisham.

4

Although the actual fighting was now over, an air of degeneration, suspicion, and a ready recourse to violence, engendered by the wars, remained to those who moved within the aura of the throne. The King, and the magnates who survived the upheaval, had lost the last remnant of the feudal ties that once bound them; mutual reliance, and even the appearance of loyalty as a moral due, were things of the past; and this was nowhere better evidenced than in the relationship between Edward IV and his brother George, Duke of Clarence, who received the manor of Bisham on the King-maker's death.

Clarence, the sixth son of Richard, Duke of York, was heir-presumptive, a prospect that played upon his mind and filled him with lofty visions of his own capacity as a plotter. His wife was Isabel, Warwick's daughter; and when her father was aiming to overthrow Edward, Clarence was false to his brother. Later he schemed with Edward against Warwick. He lent an ear to anyone, Yorkist or Lancastrian, with a grievance; but the sole outcome of his pointless treachery was a charge of high treason that brought him to the Tower.

The end of Shakespeare's "false, fleeting, perjured Clarence," in 1478, is one of those exceptional details of history known to many who otherwise care little for the past, and to many more who are unaware that the victim held the mansion house of Bisham.

It is said that Clarence was offered a choice of death. In spite of his insufficient nature, he was the sort whose easy flamboyance might well have led him to say, indicating a butt of wine such as often sustained his flights of fancy, that he was ready to be drowned in the stuff; and the gaolers took him at his word.

People of his time never doubted the anecdote, or that the wine was Malmsey; but several more recent commentators, without a shred of evidence save the urge of "realism" to support them, claim to know better.

5

One of the effects produced by the Wars of the Roses on the riverside manor of Bisham, was to increase the number of illustrious dead who were brought there for burial; and during the reign of Henry VII (1485 – 1509) the body of a young man, the last male heir of the legitimate Plantagenet line, was added to their number.

The term "legitimate" must here be stressed since the young man concerned—Edward, Earl of Warwick and Salisbury, Clarence's son—fell a victim to Henry VII, a Tudor of obscure and bastard origin who could not advance the shadow of a claim to the crown he had snatched from Richard III at Bosworth.

Edward, who had just turned ten when that occurred, was a thorn in Henry's side. But a boy of that age could not be charged with treason, the popular safeguard of shaky thrones; so Henry sent him to the Tower, trusting that some future event would enable him to remove his rival from the scene before his right could be advanced.

The chance came in a roundabout way. The full story behind it, and whether any fact may be winnowed from the fiction, can never be known. But it started with the sudden emergence on the continent of a young man who claimed to be Prince Richard of York, the second son of Edward IV, one of the two princes said to have been murdered in the Tower by their uncle, Richard III—(the progenitor of that story, and the much more likely culprit, was Henry Tudor).

The young man had much in his favour. The French Court accepted him as the legitimate King of England; so did the Dowager Duchess of Burgundy, an aunt of Prince Richard; James IV of Scotland followed suit. The young man appeared in the west of England to challenge Henry, who had it given out that the claimant was the son of a Flemish boatman, one Peter Warbeck, though, for the sake of mockery, and to add a touch of the ridiculous, Henry, like the true propagandist he was, transformed the name of Peter into Perkin.

There is another puzzling element in what followed. Perkin was arrested, but following a short spell in prison he was received at Court and there allowed to live like an honoured guest. After a while, for no apparent reason, he left his royal quarters; but this time, on being seized, he was sent to the Tower.

His cell was near that of young Edward Plantagenet. It was a common practice under the Tudors for agents, or paid informers, to visit prisoners and, by posing as their friend, to gain or manufacture sufficient evidence to secure conviction. One of these creatures (we know his name, Cleymound) visited the young men, and succeeded in luring Edward, perhaps by promising to save his life, to make some sort of confession.

Edward was declared guilty of treason, and of planning to escape from the Tower—a "crime" natural enough—with the enigmatic Perkin. A minor charge was that Edward, with the massive thickness of the Tower walls dividing them, had tapped out a message bidding Perkin be of good heart.

The latter was hanged, drawn and quartered on November 23rd, 1499; five days later Edward, aged twenty-four, was executed in the Tower, and so provided (probably because his father had held the manor) yet another of the headless bodies to lie at Bisham.

PART FIVE

Transition

1

In the succeeding reign, that of Henry VIII (1509–1547) the religious, cultural and social forces that had long been threatening to erupt in England were concentrated in a movement of unexampled proportions that changed the course of our history—the Reformation.

So far as the Bisham story is concerned, it need only be said that Henry's differences with Rome led to the suppression of the religious houses. The prime mover in this was Thomas Cromwell who, after serving Cardinal Wolsey, became chief adviser to the King.

It was he who organized the taking over of lands and properties controlled by the Church; and in July 1535 his agents, or "visitors," started on their errands of confiscation.

Two doctors of law, Richard Layton (an unsavoury character who helped to provide evidence that sent Bishop John Fisher and Sir Thomas More to the block) and Edward Carne, were entrusted with the work in the Thames Valley; and in the summer of 1536 they arrived at Bisham.

The manor house was then occupied by Margaret, daughter of Clarence, and a niece of the two Kings Edward IV and Richard III. The most likely year of her birth is 1471, and she married Sir Richard Pole, son of Geoffrey Pole whose wife, Elizabeth, was step-sister to Margaret Beaufort, the mother of Henry VII.

Geoffrey acquired the manorial rights of Medmenham,

Bucks, and dwelt there near the Cistercian Abbey. Both he and his wife were buried at Bisham.

Margaret's husband died in 1505, leaving her with five children. She was a true Plantagenet, the sister of Edward, the last male of that line, whose execution had resulted from the Perkin Warbeck affair; and in 1513 she petitioned Parliament for a restoration of the honours of her mother's family, her mother having been the King-maker's daughter Isabel.

Henry at first found Margaret, who through her father represented the right royal line, a positive embarrassment. But finding that her conduct posed no problem, he soon came to recognise her, in his own words, as "the saintliest woman in the world." His approval was confirmed by making her the governess to Princess Mary, the future Mary I; and by restoring a great part of her family estates together with the title of Countess of Salisbury. Margaret was a staunch friend of Queen Katharine, Henry's first wife.

She is mentioned in an inventory as living in the manor house of Bisham; and dating from the time of her residence there stands, near the river, a stone and flint circular dovecot, with its central post and revolving ladder, or potence, that was moved round to collect the eggs.

One of her sons was Reginald, an uncompromising champion of the Papacy who was later made Cardinal. Margaret shared his religious convictions, and she stood in the path of Layton and Carne when they arrived to order the surrender of the Austin Canons at Bisham.

The prior, Richard, was equally defiant, and Layton complained to Cromwell that he had been threatend by "my Lady of Salisbury" and others, the others being the Salisbury household backed, perhaps, by sympathisers from the village.

Cromwell settled the problem by nominating one of his "safe" men, William Barlow, who does not appear to have visited the place, as head of the priory. Barlow dutifully continued the farce by signing its surrender on July 5th. He was subsequently rewarded by being made Bishop of St. Asaph, going on from there to St. David's, then to Bath, Wells, and finally Chichester.

An astrologer might be led to conclude that the number 5 dominated Barlow's affairs. He held five sees, he fathered five daughters, and between them they married as many Elizabethan bishops.

Henry VIII was no stranger to Bisham. He had presided over his Council there; he had hunted in the woods, and gasconaded his way (he was not yet over-gross or cantankerous) through the babbling of courtiers and guests.

There is a letter dated 14th of July 1518, written at Wallingford by Richard Pace, Archdeacon of Dorset and a member of the diplomatic service, to Cardinal Wolsey, which states: "Tomorrow in the morning the King departeth to Bisham, as it is time, for they do die in these parts in every place not only of the small-pox and measles but also of the great sickness"—the plague was always at its worst in summer.

Four days later another letter from Pace, again to Wolsey, and written from "The More", near Rickmansworth, says that the King has commanded the Princess (Mary) to join him at Bisham, and to remain there until the following Tuesday. There is also an account, dated 1529, which refers to the Queen's Staff (the Queen was then Katherine of Aragon) being at Bisham for three days at a rate of tenpence a day.

It may fairly be assumed that Henry regarded Bisham with some special favour, for no sooner had the Augustinian Canons been expelled than he announced plans for re-establishing the place on a more impressive scale.

2

For that purpose the abbot and thirteen monks from the historic Benedictine house at Chertsey, Surrey, were transferred to Bisham. The move was a condition of Bisham's surrender. The Berkshire house was to receive the status of an abbey, and the abbot, William Cordrey, was granted a licence entitling him to wear the episcopal mitre.

The charter of this new foundation of the Benedictine Order was signed by Henry on December the 18th. It was given the title of the Abbey of the Holy Trinity, "out of sincere devotion to God and the Blessed Virgin His mother." The land, house and appurtenances of the former priory formed part of its endowment, with part of the thicket of White Waltham parish, together with the abbey lands of

Chertsey and Medmenham, and those of the Benedictine convent at Little Marlow—the place (already referred to) from which a nun had thought to elope when her rarely raised eyes met those of an enraptured young squire in the torchlight of the hall at Bisham, two hundred years before.

It is about this time that legend, and it may be nothing more, takes a last look at the Bisham community. This again concerns an elopement, the principals being a monk and a young woman of the district, who set off through Quarry Woods followed by the girl's father.

They took the path that runs from Marlow to Cookham Dean, and the irate pursuer, who was on a lower level, caught up with them as they came out, about midway through the woods, and where a fence now runs, on a ridge overhanging a pit or quarry. He called on them to come down, and when they refused he took aim at them with one of the clumsy firearms of the day. His shot, not surprisingly, missed its mark and wounded the girl, who died in her lover's arms.

One of Henry's purposes in founding the Abbey was coloured by a combination of reverence and sentiment. It was to be a place where prayers were said for the soul of Jane Seymour, his third and late Queen who had died in childbirth. But it was Cromwell's policy, and not Henry's, that decided the future of Bisham Abbey. For in a matter of days—ten, to be exact—Cromwell had appointed a surveyor and receiver of the Abbey lands. He was one of Cromwell's dependants, named Stydolf.

It was now obvious that Bisham, despite Henry's show of favour, would go the way of all other monasteries in the country. But Abbot Cordrey made a stand to put off the inevitable closure. He pointed out that Stydolf, who must have taken part in previous confiscations, was not in need of additional recompense, since he had received a charge of forty shillings on the late Abbey of Chertsey; and to that sum Cordrey, of his own free will, was adding a further twenty shillings yearly.

That way, and by similar shifts, the Abbey was kept in existence for another six months. But the surrender was finally enforced, and on June the 19th, 1538, the place was made over to Cromwell's agents.

It was customary for Layton to accuse his victims of vice, laziness, or luxurious living, in order to justify the process of suppression. But the reputation of Chertsey, from which the monks had been transferred, stood so high, and Bisham yielded so little in the way of possessions, that Layton could only fall back on personal disparagement.

So three days after taking, as it was called, "the assurance for the King," he wrote to Henry describing the community as being made up of "the Abbot, a very simple man, the monks of small learning and less discretion."

The inventories make it clear that the style of living maintained by the Benedictines at Bisham was even more modest than that of the Canons who preceded them. The stock consisted of "a few milch kine;" there was not a bushel of wheat, malt, or any other grain. But there was "much meadow and woodland," and the ploughmen and carters were allowed to stay on to help with the hay harvest.

The Abbey possessed very little plate and household stuff, and few vestments. There were no hangings, the walls being bare throughout; while sleeping accommodation was limited to the Abbot's bed and a mattress that was used by two of the servants. Layton was forced to borrow a bed "in the town" (which would mean Marlow) for Carne and himself.

These meagre findings led the disappointed visitor to conclude that Abbot Cordrey must have forestalled him by selling the church plate and valuables in London. He would soon, Layton went on, have sold the house and lands in order to pay for the "white wine, sugar, borage leaves and sake" (fermented liquor made from rice) "whereof he sips nightly in his chamber till midnight."

(We can follow the workings of Layton's mind in this; for later, when rewards were handed out, he became Dean of York and pawned the Minster plate).

In order to find some ready money for the monks and members of their household who were being turned upon the world, the bells and copes were sold —the latter cannot have yielded much for Layton says they were "rotten"—while the monks held an auction in the chapter-house where they sold their cowls. (The cowl is not, as commonly supposed, the hood, but a sleeveless garment that covers the head and shoulders).

One may readily believe Layton who said that the monks were anxious to be gone; but brief though their residence had been, it left a permanent reminder in that the term "Abbey" has ever since been applied to the riverside mansion house.

An account of doubtful authenticity refers to the monks, when expelled, being driven up the turret stairs, contesting every inch of the way, and to the red mark of a hand that remained impressed on the wall for years.

Henry's association with the place continued. A bill was incurred in November, 1543, for eggs and cream during Henry's stay at the Abbey; while Privy Seals show that Henry signed three documents there in the same month, and three further documents at the end of the year.

3

But although the religious foundations at Bisham were accounted for and safely delivered into Henry's hands, there remained a further disagreeable problem in the person of Margaret, "my Lady of Salisbury," who had not been silent when Cromwell's agents arrived to take over.

Henry's differences with Rome had widened into a definite breach, and as he assumed greater power and title in church affairs, so he became more intolerant of the Pole family whose religious position was unchanged.

Margaret had never concealed her disapproval of Henry's marriage to Anne Boleyn. Her son Reginald, the future Cardinal, who lived abroad, had written a book that was strongly contemptuous of Henry's claims; and with such defiance as this to enrage him, the King struck. The convenient charge of treason was invoked, and Margaret's eldest son, Henry, was executed in 1538.

In the following year Margaret was arrested and sent to the Tower. She was imprisoned for two years, and a Bill of Attainder was passed against her though she was never tried. On May the 27th, 1541, when over seventy, she was beheaded, not publicly but within the Tower precincts, being of royal blood. She was not buried at Bisham, but in the chapel of St. Peter ad Vincula, in the corner of Tower Green. In recent times she has been numbered among the *Beati* of the Catholic Church as Blessed Margaret of Salisbury.

With the monks gone, there was the usual scramble to obtain their property. Sir Richard Riche, Chancellor of the Court of Augmentations, declared that the Abbot had promised to grant him the Bisham lands; a lady named Margaret Vernon tried to lay hands on the Countess of Salisbury's house.

Both were disappointed. But the Abbey, left uninhabited for a time, took on a new lease of life following the next marriage of the King, his fourth, to a bride he had never seen, but whose beauty of face and body had been strongly recommended by Cromwell.

She was Anne of Cleves, daughter of the Lutheran Elector of Saxony; no longer young, according to the estimate of the time, being over thirty; and when Henry saw her he got such a shock that his vengeful mind began to store up a catalogue of "hates" against Cromwell that eventually brought him to the scaffold.

She was physically plain, lacking in cultural attainments, and possessed of "a glorious appetite." "Is there no remedy, but that I must needs put my neck in the yoke?" groaned Henry. He went through the ceremony of marriage with the "Flanders mare" as he called poor homely Anne, and decided that he liked her then even "much worse" than before. The marriage, never consummated, was soon annulled, and having disposed of her legally Henry relieved his mind of Anne by settling an annuity of £4,000 upon her together with several estates.

Among them was Bisham, which Anne was holding when Henry died in 1547.

It is sometimes said, without evidence, that Anne did not take favourably to Bisham. But this is contradicted by a letter she wrote, dated January the 8th, 1553, following a request made to her by Edward VI.

Anne's letter, to Princess Mary, tells how in conformity with the King's wish she was exchanging Bisham for a house in Suffolk, "with two parks and certain manors thereto adjoining." This property was owned by Sir Philip Hoby, who was Edward's ambassador to the Court of Spain. Anne then

goes on to say that had it not been for His Highness's pleasure, she would have been well content to continue without
change.

PART SIX

The Learned Family of Hoby

1

The Hobys were typical of the families who, imbued with the post-Reformation spirit of inquiring scholarship and active diplomacy, flourished during the 16th and 17th centuries. The head of the house, at the time it became prominent under Henry VIII, was William Hoby, who claimed descent from an old Radnorshire line.

Hoby was enriched by spoils that fell to certain families when the monasteries were seized by the Crown, and he later acquired, through his wife, the property of Hailes in Gloucestershire. He was described as having been "unlearned, very just and plain in his actions, and of great hospitality." He is said to have reached the age of one hundred and three.

His two marriages, first to a Howard and then to Katherine Forden, produced the sons who figure in this story; Philip born in 1505, and Thomas, who was twenty-five years his junior. In spite of the age gap between them, the brothers shared much the same tastes, interests, and talents; and at a time when even a casual cry of "Treason!" could lead one to the block, they remained cultured diplomats who kept their standing, and the monarch's favour, with only one slip.

It was made by Philip early in his career. Much of the confusion in which people of all kinds were caught up resulted from the changing ideas of religious authority and doctrine, and a vital point of discussion was, of course, the Eucharist.

The Hobys came down firmly on the side of reform, and Philip gave some support to a certain Thomas Parsons, who was said to have "evil opinions" regarding the Sacrament. This, presumably, was while a preference for tradition was battling with the urges of expedience in the King's mind; for Philip's conduct gave rise to such official displeasure that he was committed to the Fleet prison.

But his short stay there, of only six days, left him the sort of diplomat who makes safe and easy going in any weather. Never again would the throne cast a shadow in the direction of Philip Hoby; and this successful avoidance of suspicion was continued by Thomas.

One of Philip's missions was responsible for bringing a work of 16th century Flemish art to the walls of Bisham Abbey. Philip was appointed ambassador to the Court of the Emperor Charles V, then at Brussels, and in a letter dated 14th of March, 1538, from Thomas Wriothesley, Secretary of State, Philip was asked to report on any tapestries that might be of interest to the King.

A reply came from John Hutton, Henry's agent in Flanders, who, speaking for himself and Philip, said that "200 ells of goodly tapestry" had come to their notice. Hutton went on, "there has not been bought this twenty year any so good for the price," and he urged that Wriothesley, in buying it, "would have it better chepe than the stuffe was bought that it was made of."

Judged by its style it can be stated, with near certainty, that the tapestry was the work of Bernard van Orley, a Flemish artist of the time who was inspired by Raphael. That it was woven in the Belgian capital was demonstrated by such characteristic signs as the green dye, much favoured by Brussels craftsmen, and the cross woven in the salvage of one of the panels. The figures, and the scenic background, provided further evidence of the Flemish school.

The tapestry illustrates the Old Testament story of Tobias, for so long established as a favourite theme with Christian artists that its principal episodes are represented in the Roman catacombs.

Tobias (Tobie or Tobit, as he was sometimes called) was a pious believer in the ultimate providence of God. He was called on to endure great sufferings, almost to the limit of human endurance; but he held on, grimly, by a thread of faith, and so earned the reward that, he had always known, would come at the end of his trials.

The purchase of the set recommended by Hoby and John Hutton was carried through. It was found to consist of five hangings, three in good condition, one somewhat shortened, another (as it later became) partly destroyed. There is no record of where the tapestries figured on arriving in England; it may have been at Hampton Court; but later, as we shall see, they went to Bisham.

Another of Philip's early assignments was in the field of finance. The law expelling Jews from this country, passed under Edward I in 1290, was still in force; but from time to time there was evidence that money-lenders were active and regaining control of affairs.

This abuse, a tacitly accepted part of public life in our time, could then arouse popular resentment; and Philip was appointed to hold and examine "certain foreigners" who were thought to be involved in such dealings.

The affair was sufficiently important—for Henry's own estates were mortgaged—to figure in the business of the Privy Council, which also required Philip to furnish inventories of the goods, money, and other possessions owned by suspects.

In 1544 Philip put aside his gown of office and donned armour to join the English army that, as part of a plan by Henry and the Emperor Charles to embarrass their mutual enemy, France, was besieging Boulogne. When the town fell Philip was knighted; his half-brother Thomas was then in his first term at St. John's College, Cambridge.

Over the next years Philip was entrusted with missions in Spain, Portugal, and at the Emperor's Court in Brussels. When Henry VIII died in 1547 his successor, Edward VI, continued the favours shown to the elder Hoby by making him a privy councillor; while the patronage afforded by the Earl of Worcester, whose family was later connected with the Hobys by marriage, was partly responsible for Philip's steady advancement.

2

Meanwhile Thomas Hoby, who was more studious than his

brother, was maintaining his study of languages, literature, and public affairs. But continental experience was also a proper part of a gentleman's training, and the brothers travelled, sometimes together, through parts of Germany and Italy, preserving everywhere a proper balance and sense of taste however much they were ethically and culturally opposed to some of the religious reminders, monuments, and customs they encountered.

They were thoroughly at home in Strasbourg, where they stayed in the house of Martin Bucer, who was regaling university audiences with tenets of the Lutheran theology. A marked contrast was provided by Venice, the great maritime republic which was showing the first signs of running to seed, but which nevertheless struck Thomas Hoby as "the most triumphant city he ever saw."

Its wealth might have been declining, but the temper of its citizens was well in keeping with their ebullient past.

During the Hobys' stay in Venice the finale of a family feud was played out, with the members of two rival houses passing in gondolas up and down the Grand Canal, exchanging insults and threats that were only halted when one of the contestants was "shot through in many places of his body."

They heard of a quarrel that developed at the house of a lady when the Duke of Ferrandin, who "most fancied her above all the rest," found another suitor on the spot. Someone pushed roughly against the Duke and then took refuge in another room. The Duke was "shoving the door open" (the phrase is Thomas's) when an attendant crept up behind and, with a short broadsword, "clove his head in such sort as the one side hung on his shoulder by a little skin."

In describing the wound Thomas must have exaggerated a little, or perhaps the Duke was exceptionally tough, for we are told that he lived two days in that condition.

Thomas was in Rome, where there were "sundry fine antiquities to be seen," for the election of a new Pope, Julius III, in 1549. One of the cardinal-candidates for the office was Reginald Pole, a fact invested with more than normal interest for a Hoby since Pole's mother, Margaret, Countess of Salisbury, had held Bisham before being attainted.

Hoby remarks that Pole was not elected because he was

opposed by the French party. The truth is, however, that Pole was to be made Pope by acclamation, but he refused on the ground that the voting had gone in his favour by being premature.

From there Thomas went on (Philip appears to have cut short his tour) to Naples and Sicily. While at Syracuse Thomas fell in with an Englishman lately arrived from Malta, who dissuaded Thomas from visiting the island since he would find "nothing at Malta worth the sight." The brothers met at Augsburg, travelled together down the Rhine, and called at Brussels where the Emperor presented Thomas with a chain worth 1,000 crowns.

One of the posts held by Philip was that of Master of Ordnance, which meant that he was sometime in charge of the London garrison at the Tower. On one occasion, when the King made a royal progress through the county of Sussex, it devolved on Philip to provide a certain number of bows, arrows, and halberds for the men-at-arms. While at the Tower Philip was given a weekly allowance of £20 "for his diets," a high rate of reckoning which must have included those serving under him.

There are glimpses of the Hobys which show that neither of them was over strong; and the Tower, its walls damp or reeking because of the moat that encircled it, and notorious for the ravages of an east wind, increased the liver complaint and the malarial symptoms (that were then covered by the general term "ague") which often led Philip to go abroad in search of a cure.

During a period of peace and friendship with France he travelled in state, with the Marquess of Northampton, to the Court of Francis I to invest him with the Garter; and soon afterwards Philip's smooth manner was called into play when he launched a complaint to the Queen Dowager of Hungary touching some infringement of England's naval and commercial rights in waters that, since the Queen Dowager was also regent of the Netherlands, were under her governance.

In 1552 the manor of Bisham was granted to Philip in exchange for the Hoby estate in Suffolk. According to a note of thanks that Philip wrote to William Cecil, the latter was largely responsible for effecting the deal. Cecil, one of the "new men," who was destined to become chief minister and the virtual ruler of England for thirty years, was another future connection of the Hobys by marriage.

It appears that Philip held his place, with intervals between, at the Emperor's Court for several years. He was there when Edward VI died in 1553, and when Lady Jane Grey, the pitiful young victim of a plot by her unscrupulous father-in-law, the Duke of Northumberland, was put forward as queen.

During her reign of a few days, that ended on the scaffold, one of the meaningless State papers she signed was an authorisation for Philip to remain at Brussels.

The accession of Mary Tudor, an uncompromising Catholic, to the throne, might have presented Philip with a serious problem. Under her influence England made a temporary but nonetheless forceful return to the old faith. Philip's zeal for the Reformation was well known. But whatever his personal principles he was able, throughout Mary's reign and despite failing health, to stay in office. His marriage to Elizabeth (how that name recurs!) daughter of Sir Walter Stoner of Wraysbury, Bucks, proved childless.

Thomas tells us that his brother visited places "beyond the seas" for the better recovery "of a certain old disease of his." He tried the waters at Pau and at Liége. Later on Thomas decided that he too needed treatment, and the brothers together sampled the baths at Caldiero, near Verona.

3

In 1554 a noteworthy addition was made to their household at Bisham. The Queen's half-sister, Elizabeth, the daughter of Henry VIII and Anne Boleyn, a forward and accomplished young woman of twenty-one, was looked on as a rallying point for those who feared or opposed the religion and politics of Mary. The loose strands of dissatisfaction were gathered up into revolt by Sir Thomas Wyatt, the headstrong son of the poet of the same name.

He led a force from Kent into London, followed the line of the river as far as Kingston, then turned back, having failed to gain the support he had expected, for a long and useless night march back to the capital.

The rebels were badly mauled by the Queen's men at what is now Hyde Park Corner, and the broken Wyatt struggled on, with a handful of followers, to the city. He was executed. Suspicion turned naturally on Mary's rival, Elizabeth, who kept her nerve and with tongue in cheek denied all knowledge of the rising. Already she could, as the French ambassador said, "act any part she pleases."

Mary appeared to believe her; nonetheless, she adopted a mild precaution by placing Elizabeth under supervision, first at the Tower, then at Greenwich, at Hampton Court, and in the country at Hatfield and at Woodstock in Oxfordshire.

One of her custodians during that period was Sir Henry Bedingfield, a member of the Privy Council. Later she passed into the care of Lady Cecil and Lady Bacon, both of whom were familiar with the Hobys and their Berkshire home.

Now it may have been that the two ladies disliked the part they were called upon to play; or perhaps the ice-cold brain of Cecil, foreseeing a future with Elizabeth on the throne in place of Mary, decided it would be unwise for his wife to be remembered as one of her keepers.

At any rate, because of a plea by one or both of the ladies to be relieved of the charge, the Princess Elizabeth, at some time while she was still under suspicion, and for some unspecified period (three years are mentioned, but that is guess work) was entrusted to the care of Philip and Thomas Hoby at Bisham Abbey.

Her stay there marked a pleasant interval between the hazardous days of her youth and the ferments that waited ahead. She was attended by courtiers, visited by friends. The great chamber underwent alterations for her convenience. A bay window was built out, and a dais (since removed) was erected sixteen inches above the floor. She planted a mulberry tree that stood for years in the Abbey grounds.

The spring in the nearby fields, that had earlier been credited with miraculous healing power, provided the water for her bath; and the foundations of a small stone building, thought to have been her dressing-room, were later unearthed.

The period of partial restraint ended for Elizabeth in November, 1558, when the unfortunate Mary died; and it was soon after Elizabeth's accession, when the legend of "Good

Queen Bess" was about to begin, that Thomas Hoby visited Court.

One of the Queen's comments on her stay at Bisham has been responsible for some confusion. For she told Thomas: "If I had a prisoner whom I wanted to be most carefully watched, I should entrust him to your charge; if I had a prisoner I wished to be most tenderly treated, I should entrust him to your care."

But she also said to Sir Henry Bedingfield, touching the time that he had been her custodian: "God forgive you for the past as I do. When I have one who requires to be safely and steadily kept I will send him to you."

The similarity between the two statements has given rise to the conjecture that only one, that made to Bedingfield, is genuine; that the Queen never addressed herself in approximate terms to Thomas Hoby—from which it follows, (with inconclusive dates to back up the argument) that Elizabeth was never held at Bisham . . . Such tiresomeness dies hard.

At Easter in 1556 we find Philip Hoby inviting Cecil and his wife to make a July visit to Bisham. They were old friends. Lady Cecil's sister, Elizabeth, was to marry Thomas Hoby. But Philip, who was obviously repeating an invitation, wrote somewhat testily:

"What should stay you, I know not, but well I am assured that I have not heard one make so many promises, and perform so few. Peradventure my Lady stayeth you, who you say cannot ride; thereto will I provide this remedy, to send her my coach, because she shall have the less travail thither, and you no excuse to make. Let me know by this for when I shall look for you at Bisham, that my coach may come for her, for otherwise if you come not there will chance a greater matter than you yet know of. Make my commendations to your Lady, I pray you, and till I see you at Bisham, I bid you both farewell."

Meanwhile the brothers were forming plans to substantially rebuild and make additions to the Abbey. The work, which was put in hand some time prior to 1557, was on lines envisaged largely by Philip; and it adds nothing to either brother's reputation to find that they thought it necessary to demolish the priory and its church.

Dovecot dating from the time of
Margaret, Countess of Salisbury

Interior of the dovecot with the
original potence or revolving ladder

East side of the Abbey showing Elizabethan
oriel window and remains of the cloisters

Portraits of Sir Edward Hoby and
his sisters, Elizabeth and Anne

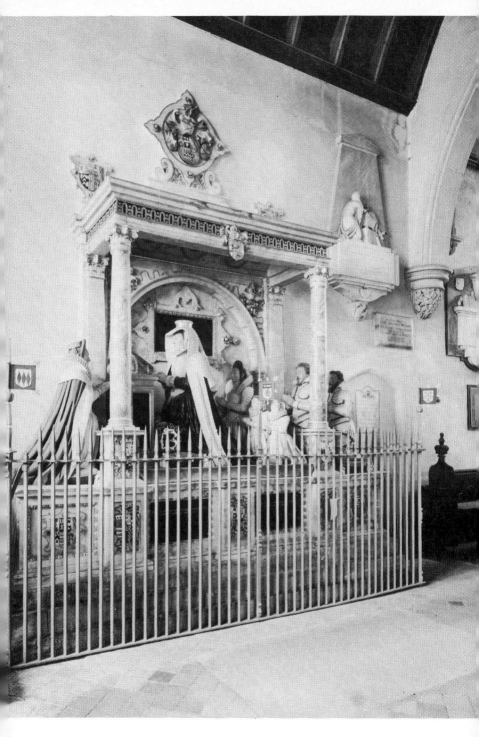

Group of Lady Hoby and her
family in All Saints' Church, Bisham

Tomb of the brothers Sir Philip and Sir
Thomas Hoby in Bisham Church

George Vansittart who purchased the
Abbey in 1780

Henry James Vansittart-Neale (1842–1923) and his
sister Henrietta (1838–1879)

Both places had been left in a sorry state by Henry's agents; and the Hobys continued the work of demolition with a thorough, and perhaps Puritan zeal, so that not only the actual buildings but the tombs of the Earls of Salisbury, including that of Warwick the King-maker, were swept away. There is only a vague reference to tombstones having been seen much later exhibited on the floor of the Abbey hall. If so, they were broken up during subsequent alterations.

Two relics of the priory church did, however, make a surprising re-appearance. When Denchworth church, in the Vale of the White Horse, near Wantage, was restored during the middle of the last century, a brass tablet was taken up from the floor. It was inscribed with a request for prayers of "whoever may pass" for William Hyde, owner of the manor of Denchworth, and his wife Margery, both of whom died in 1562.

On the reverse side was a Norman-French inscription to the effect that "Edward, King of England, who made siege before the city of Berwick and won the battle there, and the city, on the eve of St. Margaret, in the year of grace 1333, laid this stone at the request of Sir William de Montacute founder of this house."

This tablet, commemorating the victory of Edward III and the third Baron Montacute at Halidon Hill, was apparently affixed to the foundation stone of the priory of Augustinian Canons at Bisham. A likely explanation of the tablet's appearance at Denchworth is that when the priory was demolished the brasses it contained were sold for old metal. The Hydes, or someone in their vicinity, obtained the tablet, and its reverse side, as was often done for reasons of economy, was utilised for another inscription.

The other relic is a mutilated alabaster effigy that has been identified as representing Richard, Earl of Salisbury, the King-maker's father, which at some time, and for some unknown reason, was conveyed from Bisham to Burghfield church, near Reading.

The foundations of the priory and its church could sometimes be seen when a spell of dry weather left an outline of burnt brown traced on the grass, to the north-east of the Abbey. The outline survived when the spot was given over to tennis, but it was finally lost when hard courts superseded the grass.

The Hobys used the stones from the Augustinian buildings for their renovated Abbey. Hence it came to present, besides a somewhat rambling appearance, and a frontage that has since weathered to a warm colour generally associated with the Tudors, a mixture of brick, stone, flint and chalk. But the varied materials, like the style, never appear to lack cohesion when seen against the background of trees.

The focal point is the tower raised to the west of the dining room. "This year," says Thomas, writing in his diary of 1560, "was the turret built in Bisham." Of brick and stone, it occupies a triangular place in the heart of the Abbey, and is ascended by means of a central newel staircase. From the tower platform one looks down on the Thames, glass-like and scarcely moving through the flat fields of the valley, with woods on the slopes and to the north the Chilterns rising through haze.

Only one side of the 14th century cloisters, which formerly made a quadrangle, was left standing; otherwise the work carried out by the Hobys consisted mainly of enlargements and additions. These were on the north side of the hall, and included a dining room with library above, and rooms in two storeys on the south side. Some medieval domestic painting came to light when the wall was restored.

Above the hall fireplace, which was built by the Hobys, is an imposing oak overmantel. This was given by James I, soon after his accession, to Lord Windsor, whose successor in the 19th century, the Earl of Plymouth, lived at Bisham for a time.

A window at the north end of the great chamber, where Henry VIII's Council had met, and where Elizabeth's Council was soon to meet again, is rich in stained glass, some of which, dating from the 14th century, was taken from the priory church.

The oldest coat of arms to be represented is that of William Montacute, first Earl of Salisbury; there is the quartered shield of Richard Neville, father of the King-maker; Margaret, Countess of Salisbury, is commemorated by Pole impaling the arms of Clarence, since Margaret was the daughter of George, duke of that name. A later 17th century glass recalls the younger Cecil, Robert, one of the several to be created Earl of Salisbury (although no connection of the Montacutes), and Secretary of State.

At some time the tapestries were brought to Bisham. It may be that Philip took them over on Henry VIII's death, or they may have been given by Henry, with the Abbey, to the cast-off Anne of Cleves. They were cut up and part of them attached to the walls of one of the bedrooms, where they covered a motto carved on the wall: "The covetous man rooteth up his own house."

A note on the business conducted at Bisham says that the dove-house, built by Margaret, late Countess of Salisbury, was let on lease to Thomas Weldon, the Queen's treasurer.

The work on the Abbey was but half-way through when Philip Hoby died. Frequently ill, and travelling in search of a cure, he went to Bath in the summer of 1557. In the following April Thomas mentions that his brother had gone to London, "to seek the aid of physicians," and also to make his last will and testament. On May the 29th Thomas wrote in his diary: "Departed my brother out of this life to a better, at three o'clock in the morning."

Philip was fifty-three. He died at the family house at Black-friars, and on June the 9th his body was taken, by water, for burial at Bisham. Since he had no children (his wife died two years later) the Abbey was bequeathed to his half-brother, Thomas, who was then twenty-eight. With the Abbey went such minor accessories as two flagons and eighteen spoons.

Within three weeks of Philip's funeral there was another ceremony at Bisham. This was the marriage of Thomas, on June the 27th, to Elizabeth, the third daughter of Sir Antony Cooke of Gidea Hall, Essex.

Thomas and Elizabeth were well matched in that both loved things of the mind. Roger Ascham, one of the most accomplished scholars of the age, said of Thomas that he was "in many ways well furnished with learning and very expert in diverse tongues;" while Sir Antony, who had four daughters to educate, and who had also tutored the young King Edward VI, saw to it that their training fitted them to have for their husbands "complete and perfect men."

The Compleat Gentleman, published in 1622, looked back on

the girls as having been "rare poetesses, so skilful in Latin and Greek, beside many other their excellent qualities."

They certainly married well in the worldly sense. Mildred, the eldest, became Lady Burghley, wife of the Secretary of State. Anne married Sir Nicholas Bacon and was the mother of Francis, Lord Verulam, the philosopher. The youngest, Catherine, had a good knowledge of Latin, Greek and Hebrew; while Elizabeth, besides being expert, like her sisters, in the use of the needle, skilled in the household business of hall and kitchen, and sober in religion, knew both Greek and Latin; and as Lady Hoby (Thomas was knighted by the Queen at Greenwich) she became a notable and, at times, a formidable figure in local, legal, and in Court circles.

4

From the time he began his travels abroad, about 1547, to 1564, Thomas kept a diary which records his impression of various European cities. It also throws some light on family affairs at Bisham. For instance, an entry dated November the 12th, 1559, tells how his wife Elizabeth "went from Bisham to London, and there continued three weeks in physick for her great belly," a condition that was thought to be dropsy.

However, we then read, some weeks later, that his "wief," at midnight, "was delivered of a boy," which suggests that a little of our much overrated sex instruction would not have been out of place at Bisham in Tudor times.

The boy was Edward, who was destined to become quite a figure. Then came Elizabeth, born in 1562, who was followed by Anne, born 1564. Both little girls shared in the high mortality rate that was then quite common for children by dying within a few days of each other in 1570.

The notes Thomas kept remained in manuscript until they were published, many years later, as *The Travels and Life of Sir Thomas Hoby, Knight, of Bisham Abbey, written by Himself*. But the work for which he became much better known was a translation of *Il Cortegiano* (the Book of the Courtier), written by Count Baldassare Castiglioni who was the Bishop of Avila and Papal Nuncio to Spain, and who died in 1529.

Thomas's translation, on which he worked while in Paris,

was published by William Seres, at the Sign of the Hedgehog. Its success was immediate. It ran through four editions, and was praised by Roger Ascham who said that "a year's study of it, in England, would do a young man more good than three years' travel in Italy."

Divided into four books, it studied the aspects of courtesy that went to the making and bearing of a high Renaissance gentleman-scholar. It influenced many leading characters and artistic creations of the time—Shakespeare dipped into it for personal trimmings—and there was widespread agreement with the book's "puff" which described it as being "very necessary and profitable for young gentlemen and gentlewomen abiding in Court, palace, or place."

Besides being full of classical allusions and comparisons, the book is much concerned with the treatment and the conduct of women, and (never more timely than now) it points out the folly of those "silly pore creatures" who try to make themselves resemble men.

Thomas's diplomatic life was spent at the Court of Henry II in France, to which he was appointed soon after being knighted. He and Lady Hoby rode from London to Dover. The weather was bad, much rain had left the roads wet and slippery; soon after leaving Sittingbourne his wife fell from her horse; and since the lady had a temper, there must have been no little commotion when she landed in the mud.

Their discomfort was increased by a rough crossing to Calais, and to make matters worse their cavalcade, as it approached the town gate, was fired on by some French soldiers on duty there.

No one was hit, but at least one shot passed through the flag that preceded the English party. Thomas, who had his full share of the national pride that was then proper to men of every kind, demanded an apology and saw that the offender was punished; and the dignity of his office was again called into play when he presented his credentials to the French King.

Henry, surrounded by his suite, spread out the papers to read. While doing so the Cardinal of Lorraine looked over the King's shoulder, and also read the letters. His raised eyebrows and curling mouth managed to convey to Thomas, as he did so, that he detected some imperfection in the terms or in the wording; and this so angered Thomas that he stepped out of place and stood between the King and the Cardinal, thus putting an end to the superior smile by which the latter expressed his slighting estimate of the English ambassador.

The Hobys accompanied the Court when it moved to Châteaubriant, in the Chère valley, where the highly delicate political round was exchanged for hunting, shooting, the unsophisticated tennis of the day, and the game of palla malla (which afterwards gave its name to Pall Mall). Thomas's heart was gladdened when, at an exhibition of wrestling, England was represented by a team of champions from Cornwall.

Back in England for a while, Thomas had charge of the arrangements for the landing and reception of Mary of Guise, the French wife of James V of Scotland and the mother of Elizabeth's rival, Mary, Queen of Scots. This entailed much river travel to and from Hampton Court, and as a result Thomas developed "a quartan ague"—the complaint that had plagued his brother Philip—and which now "held" Thomas, as he says, "for a good space after."

For some time Thomas was afflicted by a succession of illnesses that, in addition to minor failings, were serious enough to merit a mention in his diary. For instance, at Christmas 1557, he records falling sick "of a burning fever which held me until twelfth day." Some time later he "fell sick of a sore pleurisy," and after that he "entered into a sickness' that continued with him for the space of three weeks.

He was back in Paris by 1566, and in the summer his illness took so deadly a turn that some thought he had been poisoned, a fate not uncommon for those who moved in the perilous sphere of 16th century politics. But Thomas was not engaged in any dealings momentous enough to call forth really dangerous opposition.

His last letter was dated June the 21st, 1566, and on July the 13th he died, aged thirty-six. Lady Hoby, as directed in his will, transported his body and their household effects to Bisham, a business that occupied twenty-eight days and incurred so many costs that Lady Hoby's inbred sense of economy must have been shocked by the long bill with which she was presented.

Back at Bisham a second son, born to Lady Hoby after Thomas's death, was given the appropriate name of Thomas Posthumous.

5

There are indications that Lady Hoby, who as time went on developed a most forceful and determined character, took pleasure in assuming the rôle of a defenceless woman. She did, in fact, remain a widow for eight years; then, at the age of forty-six, on the day before Christmas Eve 1574, she married, at Bisham church, Lord John Russell, son of Francis, fourth Earl of Bedford.

Lord Russell, who remains a shadowy figure, died ten years later. He was buried in Westminster Abbey, and his widow who, like many women, was fascinated by funeral trappings, indulged her fancy and, at the same time, her literary bent, by writing an inscription for his tomb. Her grief was equalled by her disappointment at Lord John having predeceased his father, the Earl, and so not succeeding to the Bedford title.

As Lady Russell (though she is better known as Lady Hoby, by which name we will call her), and also the sister-in-law of the powerful Lord Burghley, she took it upon herself to pull strings for those who needed some favour or a step forward in their career.

At such times she reminded those of her relatives whom she approached that she was "poor but proud" (proud she certainly was), "plain dealing," or "honest," while to nephews and nieces she was an aunt who "deserved the best." Cecil must have grown tired of recognising her hand on the letters that reached him from Bisham. Her constant importuning did not mean that she was inordinately kind, but rather that she was pleased to be regarded as an influential woman who counted for much.

It was then customary for books or music to be dedicated to some influential person whose name promoted the work; and Lady Hoby afforded patronage to John Dowland, the composer of lute songs and dances.

Her son Edward, by her first marriage, was following the usual course of his kind by combining the parts of courtier and diplomat with a cultural interest in literature and languages. He passed from Eton to Trinity College, Oxford, where, as a gentleman-commoner, he had as servitor the dramatist Thomas Lodge, author of *Rosalynde*.

After a period of continental travel he became popular at Court. He figured in missions that were normally entrusted to more mature men—his mother was doubtless behind him —and at the age of twenty-two he married Margaret Carey, the daughter of Lord Hunsdon.

This Lord Hunsdon was the son of Henry VIII and Mary Boleyn. Mary had been Henry's mistress for a time before that monarch's roving eye had lighted on the more elusive attraction of her sister, Anne Boleyn. Hunsdon was therefore first cousin to Queen Elizabeth, who made him Lord Chamberlain, a Privy Councillor, and Captain of the Band of Pensioners.

Elizabeth, who probably had to swallow down her resentment of Margaret Carey, showed a readiness to favour Edward by knighting him on the day following his marriage; and soon after that Edward accompanied his father-in-law on a mission to James VI of Scotland.

There is a portrait of Edward at Bisham Abbey. Painted when he was eighteen, it shows him to have been a handsome, dashing young man whose general appearance might be determined by the rakish but none the less careful tilt given to his hat. The National Portrait Gallery has another good portrait of him, aged twenty-three, showing him a little more mature but with the same characteristics.

He obviously made a favourable impression on the Scottish King, who exhibited a fulsome liking for young and personable men; and the two shared a genuine interest in theology. Nothing of this was lost upon Elizabeth, who had the same sort of darkly penetrating eye as Lady Hoby, and who, like most women whose sexual nature is perversely insufficient, was swayed by uncontrollable jealousy; and so strained did the relations between the Queen and her young courtier become that Edward absented himself from her presence, pleading as an excuse the mysterious but almost ubiquitous ague.

The cloud soon lifted, and Edward, after returning to

Court, entered Parliament. When England was threatened by the Spanish Armada he supervised and reported on part of the coastal defences, and he was present in some capacity on a Kent headland on the July night of 1588, when the lumbering galleons beat northwards to escape the fire of the lighter English vessels; while not far off, at Tilbury, his father-in-law, Lord Hunsdon, was commanding the camp of the English land forces.

Edward, in Parliament, was a fluent speaker who represented several constituencies, Berkshire in 1589 and Kent in 1592. Five years later he was given the governorship of Queenborough Castle, Isle of Sheppey, and he also became the member for Queenborough. He represented Rochester in 1603 and again in 1614. It was then illegal to export iron from England, and Edward Hoby was appointed to seek out and examine those who were suspected of breaking the law.

One of his letters, dated 7th of December 1595, contains an invitation to his cousin, Sir Robert Cecil, to what was probably the first performance of Shakespeare's *Richard II* on December the 9th.

6

The younger Hoby son, Thomas Posthumous, developed in a much less promising fashion than his brother Edward. He was physically and mentally unpleasant—or did the latter condition follow from the derision that he knew his unfavourable appearance invited from no less a person than his mother? For Lady Hoby had no mercy on those who failed to live up to her standards of proficiency, and as she watched the undersized body of Thomas Posthumous moving on his painfully thin legs she called him by nicknames that were taken up and repeated by others, "spindle-shanks," "scurvy urchin," "spindle-shanked ape." It was generally held that he was impotent.

None of his many escapades have been recorded, but one was serious enough to lead to his appearing at the Court of the Star Chamber at Westminster. The charge against him, and the impression he left upon the court, led one who was present at the case to describe Thomas as "ye busyest sawcie little Jackie in all the country."

His deeply mortified mother, hoping to rid herself of the burden, and also to knock a sense of responsibility into her rebellious offspring's head, decided to place him in the Inns of Court. But Thomas, who had no liking for law or for any kind of learning, promptly ran away. He finally turned up at Queenborough Castle, where he relied on the brotherly feeling of Edward, the governor, to give him shelter.

It appears that Thomas, wherever he went, while trying to impress others, only succeeded in making them more aware of his personal deficiencies; and in this way amused tolerance soon gave way to ridicule, as on the occasion when his antics caused him to be referred to as "the little knight that used to draw up his breeches with a shoe-horn."

We shall see later how Shakespeare was involved in a case brought by Lady Hoby over the plans for a Blackfriars playhouse; and Shakespeare paid her back by using Thomas Posthumous as model for the foolish Sir Andrew Aguecheek in *Twelfth-Night*.

But Lady Hoby's vexation was temporarily forgotten, and her abilities were brought fully into play, when in the summer of 1592 the Queen and the Court took up residence at the Abbey.

Elizabeth cannot be readily associated with little personal pleasures; but she had a genuine delight in pageantry and masques; and the villagers put aside their embroidery and lace making to witness a series of scenes, enacted by players and musicians, that were arranged to mark the royal progress down Bisham Hill.

As the cavalcade rounded the top of the hill, and looked down upon a splendid vista of the Thames winding through fields in the valley below, the silence of the trees was broken by a fanfare of trumpets. This heralded the appearance of a character who, probably on account of his being attired in skins, was described as a "wild man," though he was civilised and articulate enough to utter a speech of welcome.

This was couched in the grossly flattering terms that were almost universal in greeting the Queen's appearance; and the panegyric was repeated further down the hill where a figure representing Pan was discovered in conversation with a couple of girls, one of whom was sewing a sampler while the other tended sheep.

The cavalcade halted for the Queen to hear what passed between the girls (who, before being chosen for the masque, had satisfied the organisers that they could be described as virgins), and the rural god.

"We attend a sight more glorious than the sun rising."

"What, does Jupiter come this way?"

"No, but one that will make Jupiter blush as guilty of his unchaste jugglings. This way cometh the Queen of the Island, the wonder of the world, and nature's glory; leading affections in fetters, virginity's slaves: embracing mildness with justice, Majesty's twins.

"To her we wish as many years as our fields have ears of corn, both infinite, and to her enemies as many troubles as the woods have leaves, all intolerable."

The addresses extolling the virtues and the beauty of the poor unfortunate woman (whose skin was like parchment and who had been bald as a coot for thirty years) were repeated at the bottom of the hill, where a decorated harvest cart was drawn up. From it alighted Ceres, the Roman corn goddess, and a quartet of nymphs, who performed a rustic dance and placed on the Queen's head a crown of wheat ears set with a jewel. They sang as they did so:

"Swell Ceres now, for the gods are shrinking,
Pomona pineth,
Fruitless her tree:
Fair Phoebus shineth
Only on me.
"Conceit doth make me smile whilst I am thinking
How every one doth read my story,
How every bough on Ceres lowereth,
Cause heaven plenty on me poureth,
And they in leaves do any glory,
All other gods of power bereaven,
Ceres only Queen of heaven.

"With robes and flowers let me be dressed,
Cynthia that shineth
Is not so clear:

Cynthia declineth
When I appear.

"Yet in this isle she reigns as blessed,
And every one at her doth wonder,
And in my ears still fond fame whispers
Cynthia shall be Ceres mistress;
But first my car shall rive in sunder.
Help Phoebus, help, my fall is sudden;
Cynthia, Cynthia, must be sovereign."

And so they came to the drive admitting to the Abbey, where Lady Hoby and her son Edward received their guests. Later, in the Hall, speeches written by John Lyly in honour of the Queen were delivered. Lyly was, of course, the poet and dramatist whose work *Euphues* added a new term, euphuism, meaning high flown or artificial language, to the English tongue.

7

In that same August the Privy Council, then the all important organ of government, met at Bisham. The Council comprised the Lord Treasurer, the Lord Admiral, a certain Mr. Wolley or Wooley, and Robert Cecil. That Cecil, an ugly big-headed dwarf whom Elizabeth called "her pigmy," and whose appearance in his "great fox-furred gown" was ridiculed in lampoons, was the son of William Cecil, Lord Burghley; and Robert, as his father had done, took over the ruling of England in the Queen's name.

The State papers of the Privy Council give us some idea of the national, domestic and household business that was conducted at Bisham. The Queen stayed at the Abbey for six days on the occasion of the masque; and there is an account of the audit office, made out to Richard Brakenbury, gentleman-usher of Her Majesty's chamber, for the allowance due to herself and to three yeomen, one yeoman usher, two grooms of the chamber, and two grooms of the wardrobe, for having prepared the Abbey in readiness for the visit.

Another audit office account upon a warrant signed by the Lord Treasurer refers to the payment of Richard Mullard, servant to the Earl of Bedford, for bringing letters from Mr. Bodley, the Queen's ambassador at the Hague, to the Court at Bisham. Another account is made out for Edward Bate, who carried letters concerning the Queen's special service from Calais to Bisham.

Among the petitions dealt with was one from Jeffrey Caswell, "a distressed mariner of Exmouth," whose trouble, pecuniary or otherwise, was sufficiently grave to merit his applying to the Council for protection, which was granted. There was also the case of Thomas Martin, a London merchant, who was "in difficulties;" and of John Eccleston, a gentleman of Lancashire, who had suffered some lawlessness or damage at the hands of a neighbour, Richard Williams.

A more outstanding problem had a typical Elizabethan flavour. A number of sailors had volunteered to take part in a new raiding expedition against Spain that was to be led by the seaman-coloniser and man of letters Sir Walter Raleigh. But when they were almost on the point of sailing the Queen discovered that one of her maids-of-honour, Elizabeth Throckmorton, was expecting a child.

That alone was sufficient to inflame the outraged morality of the Virgin Queen; and when it was known that the dashing Raleigh was responsible for the girl's condition, Elizabeth's anger was such that the expedition, although it might have brought her financial profit, was called off.

It is easy to picture the scene as the payment of the disappointed seamen was settled by those meeting about the Council table at the Abbey—the Queen seizing the occasion to give renewed vent to her indignation against Raleigh and the girl who had forfeited her title as maid-of-honour; the Lord Admiral and the rest putting pen to the necessary documents; and outside the smooth lawns, the green background of Quarry Woods, and the warm August air tempered by a breeze from the river.

The following extract from the Domestic State Papers, dated from Bisham on the 14th of August 1592, shows that all was not yet well with the newly established national Church. It was addressed to the Earl of Huntingdon, who was Lord Lieutenant and also Lord President of York, and it called upon him to exercise tighter control on religious matters that came under his notice.

"Her Majesty understanding the defection in religion which has lately grown after so long experience of God's mercy . . . attributes the fault to overmuch leniency shown to such as wilfully refuse to go to church . . . and thinks it expedient that the principal of the obstinate persons within his Lordship's jurisdiction be secured in some place of strength within the county . . . and that some discreet persons of ability and good disposition in religion do take charge of them."

This letter was signed by the Lord Keeper, the Lord Treasurer, the Lord Admiral, Lord Cobham, and, of course, by the omnipotent Robert Cecil.

8

While spending most of her time at Bisham, Lady Hoby still maintained the family establishment at Blackfriars. As time went on, the sternly moral and censorious dame was becoming well known in Court and in legal circles. She was ready to rush to law on the slightest pretext, and those concerned in her cases knew in advance that they were booked to encounter a positive Tartar.

In the summer and autumn of 1593 trouble developed between her and a neighbour, Mr. Lovelace, who lived at Ladye Place, Hurley, a residence he had built on the site of a Benedictine monastery, on the same side but a little way up stream from Bisham.

It may be that Lovelace, whose fortune derived from the sacking of a Spanish fleet in the West Indies, lacked something of the fine Hoby tradition as exemplified by the brothers Philip and Thomas. At any rate, Dame Hoby declared that two of his men had "behaved lewdly" towards her; and whether the incident was trifling or serious, she took the law into her own hands, and had the offenders seized and placed in the stocks.

Lovelace, in spite of being a justice of the peace, proved equally truculent. Some twenty of his servants, armed with halberds and long poles, marched on the Abbey, and after breaking into the porter's lodge they released the men.

In framing her complaint, Lady Hoby demanded that

Lovelace should cease to function as a justice and be "put out of the commission of the peace." That had the effect of spurring Lovelace, who was obviously ill natured, to an act of petty annoyance. It was known that Lady Hoby had placed certain of her belongings, under lock and key, in the tower at Windsor Castle, and that she had expressly forbidden anyone to tamper with the tower or its contents.

Lovelace showed his defiance of her wishes by sending one of his men to change the lock; and Lady Hoby, who delighted to pose as a suppliant, and who now described herself as "a woman who depended upon God and Her Majesty," took the case to court.

The conflicting evidence, vigorously pressed by both sides, so embarrassed the Attorney-General, Sir Edward Coke, that he fell back upon the time honoured refuge of legal minds in a quandary by binding Lovelace over until such time as the matter could be more closely examined. It never was.

Lady Hoby was next in trouble at her residence in Blackfriars. The district was much favoured by some of her own social circle, including Lord Hunsdon and Lord Cobham, and its religious tone was predominantly Low Church. It therefore came as a shock to them to learn that Richard Burbage, tragedian and associate of Shakespeare, had taken the refectory and upper part of the old Dominican priory, at the west end of Carter Lane, with the purpose of converting the premises into a playhouse.

On hearing of this threatened invasion, Lady Hoby and nineteen other property owners in Blackfriars presented a petition to the Privy Council. It was alleged that the opening of a playhouse, by encouraging vagabonds, lewd persons, and playgoers (since audiences were damned as surely as the actors) would prove such an annoyance that the tone of the neighbourhood would decline. Furthermore, since theatres then opened on Sunday, the blare of trumpets and beating of drums would seriously interfere with church services.

The Council were sympathetic to the protest and banned the playhouse. But Burbage, whose legal adviser was well versed in pettifogging twists, was afterwards given the necessary permit after pleading that he meant to convert the premises into a private house.

About this time Lady Hoby was relieved of what was perhaps her greatest personal worry. For in the month of August her problem son, Thomas Posthumous, surprised his friends and relations, and maybe himself most of all, by getting married.

He had never lived up to the state that was proper to one of the Hoby family—his kind are frequently careless and his mother was a rigid disciplinarian who kept a tight hand on money; but now he was suddenly made free since his bride, Margaret Dakins, was the heiress daughter of an East Riding magnate whose wealth was in land.

The atmosphere of the wedding, at Blackfriars, was definitely Low Church. Not a chord of music was heard, there was none of the usual dancing; instead the guests, who remained seated when dinner was over, were treated to a lengthy sermon.

The couple settled at Hackness, near Scarborough. The local tenantry, anxious to catch a glimpse of their future landlord, were not in the least impressed when Thomas Posthumous arrived with his coach and three horses; for, as one stolid Yorkshireman observed, the whole lot "was hardly worth sixpence."

The ferocious little fellow was soon spreading annoyance wherever he went. His main occupation (which must have gone some way to smoothing his mother's feelings towards him) was to seek out and persecute Papists who refused to attend the national Church. The county of Yorkshire was notorious as a hotbed of recusants, and Thomas was kept busy.

He died in 1640 at the age of seventy-four, leaving, as his most consistent legacy, the reputation of having been a plague to the district. His wife's diary, published in 1930, gives an early and most interesting account of life at one of the lesser Elizabethan-Jacobean manors.

Lady Hoby decided that it was high time for her daughter Anne Russell, who was then twenty-two, to be married, and casting a critical eye over the young men of their circle it lighted upon Lord Henry Herbert, a son of the Earl of Worcester. The match presented no great difficulty, as the Earl was by no means wealthy, but Lady Hoby enlisted the support of Robert

Cecil in promoting the marriage, pointing out that Anne would bring a comfortable dowry and that the Earl had a modest income and a great many children.

The marriage took place in 1597, and once again the party was celebrated at the Hobys' London house. But this time it was marked by none of the half measures that had rendered Thomas's marriage such a mean affair. Anne was Elizabeth's god-daughter and one of her attendants, but even so the presence of the Queen as a guest, and the arrival of Lady Hoby with a retinue of eighteen coaches, caused the ordinary residents of Blackfriars to open their eyes and declare that never before had such regal state attended a maid-of-honour.

Few celebrations were then complete without a masque, and after supper some of the ladies, each representing a Muse, entertained with a series of scenes and a dance. The Queen was persuaded to trip a measure, and the dance was led by Mary Fitton, commonly supposed to have been Shakespeare's "Dark Lady of the Sonnets." She was there in the character of Affection, and among her followers was the bride's younger sister, Elizabeth Russell. The dress of the dancers was a silver skirt and a rich bodice worked with gold and silver threads. Their hair, worn on the shoulders, was "curiously knotted."

But however privileged their position, the Elizabethans could seldom claim more than a tenuous hold on the life that for them was represented by pageantry, music and verse; and in little over a week the body of poor young Elizabeth Russell was being prepared for the family vault at Bisham.

Between these activities, the legal cases in which she was involved, and the cares of estate management, Lady Hoby was pursuing her interest in literature and theology. She produced an English translation of a French Protestant treatise, which was duly published in 1605 under the title of *A Way of Reconciliation touching the true nature and substance of the Body and Blood of Christ in the Sacrament.*

Her physical state was declining. She was troubled by the cold, and wrote in one of her letters that, in spite of wearing long clothes, the least wet affected her feet and legs, making her head "so subject to rheum" that she became deaf and quite unfit for any company.

9

During that same year, 1605, Edward Hoby and his wife were entertaining at Bisham. In a letter addressed to Thomas Edmunds, English minister at Brussels, Edward refers to a Belgian lady who was making a favourable impression in Court circles.

He states: "I hear that Madame de Hoboquens was with the Queen"—(Anne of Denmark, wife of James I)—"at Hampton Court, where she did excellently carry herself, to her great commendation. I have not yet seen her, but will do so with the first opportunity I can, and will do her all the honour and service I can . . ." His intention was realised when, some weeks later, Madame de Hoboquens visited the Hobys at Bisham.

Before the end of the year Edward's wife, Margaret, died and was buried at Bisham. He was married a second time to Elizabeth, daughter of Sir John Danvers. She died some years later, and was buried near Margaret. Edward was married a third time to Cecile, daughter of Sir Edward Unton, a Berkshire squire. There was no child (at least, no surviving one) of either marriage, though before Margaret's death Edward had a natural son by his mistress, Katherine Pinkney, who lived within walking distance of the Abbey.

The earliest mention of her family occurs in 1199, when Simon de Pinkney acquired a manor in Cookham parish. The holding came to an end in the mid-15th century, but their name lives on in Pinkneys Green, between Bisham and Maidenhead.

The Bisham parish register, under date of April the 10th, 1611, records the burial of Robert Hoby, son of Sir Edward Hoby, though the last five words were afterwards erased; and it was Peregrine, the son of Edward and Katherine Pinkney, who was named Edward's heir at Bisham.

Edward's pen was kept busy in translating .works from the French and Spanish languages, and in cultivating the friendship of scholars such as William Camden, the traveller-historian. The latter, in his *Britannica*, praised Edward's learning, and Camden's chronicle *Hibernia* was dedicated to Edward.

The old notions of battle were being transformed by the wider use of gunpowder, and one of Edward's translations, from the Spanish, was on the theory and practice of war. But Edward's most natural outlet was in the field of religion, where tracts endorsing every aspect of Protestant theology, and some even Catholic, were issuing from the press.

Their titles, and the furious sallies to which the authors treated each other, are far more entertaining than their matter. The ball was set rolling by a pair of Papists, Theophilus Higgons and John Fludd, with their outburst, *The Overthrow of the Protestants Pulpit Babel*.

Edward struck back with *A Counter-Snarl for Ishmael Rabshachel, a Cecropidan Lycnonite*. Higgons and Fludd responded in *Purgatory's triumph over Hell, maugre the barking of Cerberus in Sir Edward Hoby's Counter-Snarl;"* and Edward replied in *A currycomb for a coxcomb, in answer to a lewd libel lately foricated by Jabal Rachil against Sir Edward Hoby's Counter-Snarl . . ."* The road to salvation called for very heavy going in those days.

10

Meanwhile Sir Edward's mother, at the age of seventy-eight, was continuing to make her presence felt in matters that concerned the rights and privileges with which, she claimed, she had been invested over the years. One of these concerned the office of keeper at Donnington Castle, near Newbury in Berkshire.

This office, together with a grant of ninepence-halfpenny a day, had been made over to Lady Hoby in 1590 by the Queen. But a few years later Elizabeth, without informing the old dowager, had transferred the manor and castle of Donnington to Charles Howard, Earl of Nottingham and the Lord High Admiral, for life. But Lady Hoby refused to hand over the castle. So matters stood at the time of Elizabeth's death, in 1603, and the accession of James I.

Lady Hoby was visiting her daughter Anne, Lady Herbert, in Wales when she heard that the Lord Admiral had moved in and taken possession of the castle. She at once journeyed to the spot, and although she asserted her original claim the presence of the Admiral's men prevented her gaining entrance.

She thereupon returned to her carriage, which was at the castle gates, and sat there all night, a living remonstrance nursing her indignation until she could vent it on a local justice of the peace, whom she summoned early in the morning.

The rights and wrongs of the case were beyond him, and Lady Hoby took her grievance to the Court of the Star Chamber, where it was heard on May the 14th, 1606. It was not clear whether the Lord Admiral had been correct in claiming immediate entry, or whether his term as keeper was meant to run from the time of Lady Hoby's death.

She listened with obvious impatience to the drawn out proceedings, and just as the judges were ready to deliver their verdict her temper overcame her. She rose to her feet, protesting that she was in the right, and although various lords tried to silence or restrain her she stood her ground.

Her voice dominated the court for more than thirty minutes. Her counsel, overcome with embarrassment by her "very bold and stout manner," as an observer put it, left the bar. The Earl of Nottingham tried to intervene, but she seized him by the cloak, declaring that he was ignorant of the law and that the points he attempted to raise "were otherwise before he was born."

That little diversion apparently gave her a new vigour, for she returned to the attack and emphasized the rights that had been vested in her by Elizabeth. The Lord Chancellor tried to break in, but failed. The Lord Treasurer, and the body of lords present, were likewise repulsed. It is therefore hardly to be wondered at that she lost the case and was ordered to pay costs.

Apart from litigation, a love of funerals, with the show and solemnity involved, was deeply rooted in Lady Hoby's nature. She had seen two husbands and several of her children taken to their last resting places; and now she took a hand in preparing a monument for her daughter-in-law Margaret, who died in 1605.

The memorial to her is a strange affair. It consists of an obelisk with a swan, the Carey family crest, at each of the corners. On top of the obelisk is a flaming heart, and the inscription runs, "Never mother and the best wife." Edward, as already mentioned, contracted two other marriages, so he had ample opportunities for retaining or retracting his appreciation of Margaret.

As part of her plan to honour her first husband and his brother, Lady Hoby carried out extensive alterations in the mid-12th century church. She removed a wall of the chancel, and on the south side of the church she erected the Hoby chapel, where effigies of the two knights rest side by side (Philip is near the wall) on an imposing alabaster tomb.

They are short-bearded, majestic men, in the full armour and trappings of the time, with every strap, hinge and buckle of their gorgets and breastplates, their tassets covering the thighs, and ornamental ribbons, so faithfully reproduced as to satisfy the most meticulous armourer. Their heads are resting on their helmets, and at their feet (they are eminently square-toed) is a falcon or hobby hawk, intended as a play on the family name. Three such hobbies figure in the family arms.

Included on panels on the face of the tomb is the Hoby shield, with epitaphs and laudatory verses in Latin, Greek and English. The English verses begin:

"Two worthye knightes and Hobies both by name
Enclosed within this marble stone do rest . . ."

The obituary, also in verse, is by an anonymous "T. B.," while Lady Hoby, whose pen was always ready to dash off funeral lines, had concluded her lament for Thomas with these words:

"Give me, O God! a husband like to Thomas,
Or else restore me to my husband Thomas."

We have seen how Providence chose to avail itself of the first injunction by providing the personable Lord John Russell.

The most frequently quoted of Lady Hoby's letters is one that she addressed to Sir William Dethick, Garter King-at-Arms. She wrote it while the funeral mood was still weighing heavily upon her, and in it she asked for details of the formalities and etiquette to be observed when the time came for escorting her body to the Hoby chapel.

What style of hearse could be employed for one of her standing—how many banners carried—what scutcheons and hangings could be displayed in the church—and what were the proper funeral offerings? How many lords, gentlemen-ushers, heralds and pages could walk in the procession? She wished to arrange for her obsequies in advance so that nothing in the way of correct and elaborate detail might be neglected; and she pressed Mr. Garter to inform her of these things exactly, for she was aware of warnings that were bidding her "to prepare a pickaxe."

The memorial to Lady Hoby and her children is to the west of the brothers' tomb. There she is depicted kneeling at a prie-dieu, wearing her weeds, and a wimple so elaborate that the coronet surmounting it appears to be in danger of toppling.

Kneeling before her is her daughter, Anne, Countess of Worcester. She is robed as a peeress, with a ruff and a roll of hair so abundant that here again the coronet it supports appears but a miniature ornament.

Behind Lady Hoby, and also kneeling, are two daughters of her first marriage, Elizabeth and Anne, both of whom died young in 1570. A daughter of her second marriage, another Elizabeth, kneels by the wall. The two Hoby sons, Edward and Thomas Posthumous, are behind the girls. It is only by being somewhat small that Thomas in any way justifies the contemporary descriptions of him.

A tiny figure, with his feet emerging from a swathe of petticoats, occupies an unusual position on the floor by Lady Hoby. This represents the first child of her second marriage, Thomas, who died at a very early age. The group of tight-waisted females, and the two neatly bearded men, all exemplifying by their gestures the pious Puritan ideal, kneel under a canopy.

A final dignity was added to the chapel by a display of banners and coats of arms including those of the Hobys, the Russells, and the Cookes of Gidea Hall, the old dowager's family. A shield commemorates the marriage of her sister Mildred to Lord Burghley; while overlooking them all is a splendid armorial window of enamelled glass erected by Sir Edward Hoby in memory of his parents and his wife.

The completion of the Hoby memorials provided a link between the great volume of stone by the riverside, where first the Templars had come with the glory of the Crusades fresh upon them, and its more humble parish neighbour of All Saints; and early in June 1609, having reached the age of eighty-one, Lady Hoby was carried from the Abbey to the

church, the central subject in one of the solemn processions
that had given her such morbid satisfaction.

11

It now remained for Sir Edward to carry on the Hoby traditions at Bisham. But though he remained in royal favour—his
friend James I made him a groom of the Privy Chamber, and
he was granted an exclusive and profitable licence to purchase
wool in Warwick and Staffordshire—there is little beyond a
round of hospitality and entertainment to mark his holding of
the manor.

James I and his Queen, Anne of Denmark, were in residence at the Abbey in August 1610. On September the 3rd,
1612, James was again there for the night. An exchequer
account dated August, 1616, refers to the Abbey being made
ready for James, who was then due to stay there for eight
days, at a cost of £7.17.3d. Royal progresses from county to
county had for long been an established part of the sovereign's
commitment, and in 1617 James made an extended tour
through England and Scotland. On his way back to London
he made a point of visiting the Abbey, and as he approached
the village the bells of Marlow and other neighbouring
churches pealed a welcome.

Sir Edward died at Queenborough Castle in 1617, and his
body was carried to the Hoby family vault. He was followed at
the Abbey by his natural son, Peregrine, who married Catherine, daughter of Sir William Dodington of Breamore, Hampshire; and during their time Charles I was entertained at
Bisham.

The Calendar of State Papers contains an entry for July the
25th, 1625, drawn up by Lord Conway, secretary to George,
Duke of Buckingham: "The King has further commanded me
to let you know that by reason of the sickness coming to
Windsor he goes upon Wednesday to Woking and on Friday
to Bisham." Four days later the secretary wrote to his son, Sir
Edward Conway: "This night, with the Court, I lie at
Bisham."

Peregrine was either a man who genuinely changed his
views, or a political trimmer who veered according to the

wind. For after holding an important office under the Round-
heads, he was knighted by Charles II when monarchy was restored.

Of the six children of Peregrine's marriage, his eldest son,
Edward, was created a baronet in 1666. Sir Edward's
daughter, Elizabeth, married Henry, fifth Earl of Sterling.
Meanwhile Peregrine had settled for a political career, and
represented Marlow in the parliaments of 1640 and 1660.

Peregrine and his wife, their son Edward, and Elizabeth,
Countess of Sterling, who died at the age of twenty-seven in
1694, were all buried at Bisham.

After Peregrine, the Hoby line drew to a quietly inauspi-
cious close. The last male holder of the name was the Very
Reverend Sir Philip Hoby, who was Dean of Adfert and
Chancellor of St. Patrick's, Dublin. He died in 1766, without
issue, and the Abbey passed to his maternal first cousin, Sir
John Mill. During his time, in the December of 1768, the river
rose so high that flood water reached to the pulpit of the
church; and on two occasions divine service was held in the
Abbey.

Sir John, who obtained the permission of Parliament to
prefix the name of Hoby to Mill, died in 1780, also without
issue. It seems something of an anomaly to come upon the
ledger stone marking his place of burial in the Hoby chapel, as
also does the fact that his widow placed the old home of the
Templars in the property market.

PART SEVEN

A Home of Ancient Peace

1

An incident that was to add a fresh chapter to the Bisham Abbey story occurred on April the 19th, 1760, when George Vansittart, a fifteen-year old pupil at Reading School, took up his pen to write a letter to a friend, Doctor John Loveday, who lived at Caversham.

The letter, a typical example of that socially artificial time, began thus:

"Sir, I will not ask your advice in a matter which is already determined, nor desire to know your opinion with a resolution not to take it unless it falls in with my own, but freely declare to you that I shall go the the East Indies, and give you my reasons for doing so.

"In the first place my father and mother desire it. I have reason to think that both of them, or at least the latter, would be much grieved if I was not to go.

"Now I think it by no means the part of a dutiful son to give any uneasiness to those from whom he has received so many benefits if he can well avoid it. Secondly, if things continue in that part of the world in the same situation as they are at present, I may reasonably expect to get a handsome fortune in about twelve years, and then I may return to England and live the rest of my life (if I live so long) according to my own pleasure."

The letter went on to say that the writer had a brother in the East Indies "who may take care of my interests and settle me in business, and make my situation agreeable, and that he has invited me over.'' The young George felt sure that this new life would not be prejudicial to his morals, as he hoped to keep up sufficient Greek to be able to read the Testament in the original language. Failing that, he hoped to learn from the English version "as much as is necessary to salvation." He went on: "But whatever trials befall me I trust that the Grace of God with my own hearty endeavours will carry me safely through them."

The writer was the sixth son of Arthur Vansittart of Shottesbrooke House, Berkshire, and the brother referred to was Henry, who became Governor of Bengal and later Governor of Fort St. George, Madras.

George's expectations, with Henry's influence to promote them, were amply realised when he entered the East India Civil Service in the following year. He became a Senior Merchant and a member of the Council of Bengal, and filled a difficult and painstaking post for a time as Persian interpreter in the Persian and Bengalese Translator's Office.

His proficiency in those languages led to his being attached to the staff of Lord Clive—the Robert Clive who secured the foundations of the Empire in India.

In 1767 George Vansittart entered diplomatic life as Resident at Midnapore; and about that time he married Sara Stonhouse, daughter of the Reverend Sir John Stonhouse, Bart. His career was carried a step further when, five years later, he became Chief of the Revenue at Patna. Meanwhile his fortune had been steadily growing, and after playing an important part in the Bengal Council at Calcutta, and as a member of the Board of Trade, he returned to England, now able to live, as he had anticipated when a boy of fifteen, according to his "own pleasure."

That pleasure became centralised, and in concrete form when, in 1780, he purchased Bisham Abbey.

2

The name Vansittart derived from the old town of Sittart, in the province of Limburg in the Netherlands. The ancestor of the English branch of the family was living there in the latter part of the 16th century, when the effects of the Protestant Reformation were sweeping over Europe. He became a zealous supporter of reform, and before long he found it necessary to fly to Dantzic, in Poland, in order to escape the apostolic attention of the Catholic Archbishop of Cologne.

His grandson Peter, born in 1651, settled in the England of Charles II in 1670. At the age of twenty-six, when naturalized, he was a prominent city merchant, and soon launched out into becoming a merchant adventurer in the true sense. He not only organized but, as a speaker of German, Russian and Polish, he personally conducted trading expeditions to India, Russia, to the Baltic and the South Seas.

He was a director of the East India Company and a governor of the Russian Company, and it was the eldest of his six sons, Robert, who acquired Shottesbrooke House, near White Waltham, Berkshire, in 1712. Peter's fifth son was Arthur, whose sixth or youngest son was George Vansittart, the writer of the letter we have quoted and the subsequent owner of Bisham Abbey, which at that time comprised 1,650 acres and a villa called Temple House with 153 acres.

George's experience in the East caused him to be summoned as a witness during the impeachment of Warren Hastings who, after being the first Governor-General of India, was charged with cruelty and corruption. The affair lasted seven years, and Hastings was finally acquitted.

As Tory M.P. for Berkshire, and later as member for Reading, George Vansittart sat in a number of Parliaments. His local offices included those of High Steward of Maidenhead, and Captain of the Maidenhead (Infantry) Association. One of his letters, written in February 1789, summons up a picture of smoke drifting from the Abbey chimneys and lights making yellow the windows against their background of trees: "All our young folk, eight in number, have been at home this Christmas, and the old Abbey has been very warm and chearful"—(so spelt).

George Vansittart died in 1825, and he and his wife, who predeceased him six years earlier, were both buried in Bisham church.

3

Three of George Vansittart's brothers were members of the most notorious society that has ever assembled in England. This was the Hell Fire Club, founded in the mid-18th century by Sir Francis Dashwood, of West Wycombe Park, Bucks, at the then derelict Cistercian Abbey of Medmenham, some three miles upstream from Bisham.

The brothers were Henry, Governor of Bengal, who had promoted George's interests in the East Indies; Arthur, a Berkshire M.P.; and Robert, who became Regius Professor of Civil Law at Oxford. Robert presented the King, George III, with what must have been a somewhat embarrassing gift, sent over by brother Henry, consisting of a Persian mare, two elephants and a rhinoceros.

The doings of the club, the members of which were all men of substance or of some reputation, are subject to so many contradictions that few things are certain about them. Even the habits they wore for their so-called orgies have been variously described. But their main purpose seems to have been to make a mockery of religious forms, not in the serious black magic sense, as sometimes asserted, but rather to indulge an adolescent desire to shock and horrify.

They played at administering the Sacraments, recited the Lord's Prayer backwards, intoned blasphemies and sang bawdy choruses, drank quantities of claret and danced naked in the moonlight. Their meetings were graced by the appearance of the Nuns of Medmenham, some of whom were seasoned London females brought down for the occasion, while others were venturesome locals who needed a fling; and whenever the "monks," or Franciscans as they were called, were known to be in session the villagers locked their doors, put out their lights and trembled in the darkness.

Henry Vansittart had his portrait painted, by Hogarth, in the costume affected by the club; and he showed an active interest in the club's proceedings by presenting it with a rare book and an animal that can hardly be described as a pet or a mascot.

The book was a Sanscrit work that contained the teachings of Kama Sutra. It was a sexual handbook and one of the many ancient books dedicated to the worship of Venus (for sex, contrary to what its addicts believe, is not a modern discovery).

The animal was a large baboon that Henry had shipped from India. It was kept at Medmenham, and one night, when the "monks" were at their service in the Abbey chapel, the animal, attired in a black robe and with horns projecting from its head, was let loose among them.

It seemed that the master of the Pit had come to claim his own. The jumble of prayers gave way to cries of fear and supplications for pardon as the animal clung to the back of one he seemed to have selected for his special victim; and though, of course, the identity of the "fiend" was soon revealed, the incident was one of several that finally led to the club's closure.

Henry's lapse into the profane—or the ridiculous—was amply made up for by his youngest son, Nicholas, who followed so orthodox a line of conduct that he was created Lord Bexley in 1823, became Chancellor of the Exchequer, and sat as President of the British and Foreign Bible Society.

4

The eldest son of the Vansittart who purchased Bisham Abbey became a soldier. George Henry Vansittart, born in 1768, was gazetted ensign in the 19th (Royal Irish) Foot. His regiment was part of the force which, during the French Revolution, covered and aided the escape of Royalists from the seething port of Toulon.

Later, when the threat of Napoleon's invasion hung over the southern counties, he raised and commanded the 1st (Garrison) battalion of the Royal Berkshire Militia. The two colours of that battalion now hang from the minstrels' gallery in the Abbey hall. Promoted general in 1821, he died three years later. He and his wife, Anne Mary Copson, were both buried at Bisham.

His youngest brother, Henry, born in 1777, entered the navy and also served in the French Revolutionary wars. He was present at the combined naval and military operations that led to the capture of the Corsican stronghold of Calvi in August, 1794, where the impetuous little Captain Horatio Nelson lost his right eye.

He reached the rank of vice-admiral and died in 1843.

Another member of the family, Arthur Vansittart, born in 1815, although not directly connected with the Abbey, carried out a number of escapades that call for a mention. While still a schoolboy at Eton he visited Spithead, dived down to the wreck of the *Royal George* which had sunk in 1782, and came up with two bottles of claret. He proudly presented one of these to the Lords of the Admiralty.

A year or two later, while studying at Brunswick, he won a bet against some officers of the Black Hussars and electrified the audience, including the Grand Duke, at the Theatre Royal, by emitting blasts from a trombone while an entr'acte was being played. He made the ascent of Mont Blanc in (then) record time, and later again showed his prowess in the water by diving to the bottom of the Dead Sea. Even his marriage was the outcome of a sporting wager. His bride was Diana Sara Crosbin, one of the belles who invited glances at the Court of William IV; and Arthur won her by coming home first in a race from London to Brighton.

5

The Vansittarts had two family connections with Oliver Cromwell, Lord Protector of England from 1653 to 1658. The Henry Vansittart who governed Bengal married Amelia Morse, daughter of Nicholas Morse, who was Governor of Madras; and Nicholas was in the line of descent from Oliver Cromwell.

The other connection derived from the family of Neale, who had been settled in the Midlands since the time of Richard III. One of their members, John Neale, supported the Parliamentary side during the Civil War. He became M.P. for Bedfordshire, and married Anna, daughter of Henry Cromwell who was a cousin of the Protector. In 1651 Henry Neale, John's son, purchased Allesley Park, near Coventry.

Henry's grand-daughter, Anne, married the Reverend Sir John Stonhouse, Bart., and they had a daughter Sara. The girl's great-aunt, Martha Stonhouse, married Arthur Vansittart, of Shottesbrooke (1691—1760); and it was their son, George Vansittart, who married Sara Stonhouse and who purchased Bisham Abbey.

On the death of the widow of the last surviving Neale, in 1805, the Allesley estate passed to the Vansittarts. This was by way of Anne Stonhouse to her grandson, Edward Vansittart, who was born in 1769, took Holy Orders, and was for some years rector of Taplow, Bucks. It was he who added the surname of Neale to Vansittart, by sign manual.

A contemporary portrait of Oliver Cromwell, formerly at Allesley Park, used to hang in the Abbey; and while on the subject of Cromwell there is another connection with this story that is strange enough to allow for a little digression.

It began in 1864 when Henrietta Vansittart-Neale married into the family of Dickinson (the name will occur again later); and the Dickinsons had for cousins a family named Wilkinson who, since some time early in the 19th century, possessed an intimate and somewhat gruesome relic of Oliver Cromwell.

On his death in 1658 the body of Cromwell was embalmed and buried in Westminster Abbey. It was exhumed three years later when the monarchy had been restored, and dragged to Tyburn, where it hung till sunset on the gallows. It was then cut down, the head being clumsily struck off and set on a spike above Westminster Hall.

It remained there for twenty-five years until it was blown down in a storm and picked up by a soldier on duty outside the Hall. He took it home, but becoming alarmed by the outcry raised over the missing head he hid it in the chimney.

It was afterwards sold to a broken-down actor named Samuel Russell who put it on show in Clare Market. On being threatened with prison for debt, Russell sold the head to a pawnbroker-jeweller-curio-collector James Cox, who put it on exhibition in Mead Court, Old Bond Street, charging half-a-crown for admission.

The relic was then purchased for £230 by three anonymous admirers of Cromwell, and the niece of one of these entrusted it to the care of her doctor, Josiah Henry Wilkinson. It remained in his family for more than a century, during which time it passed to Canon Horace Wilkinson, the rector of Woodbridge, Suffolk.

Wrapped in silk, the head reposed in an oak chest at the

foot of the rector's bed. Mummified through embalmment, it could be readily identified as being indeed the Lord Protector's pate, with such distinguishing marks as the meeting eyebrows (the hair, beard and moustache were practically intact) and a trace of the famous mole over the right eye. The Wilkinson cat used to sleep on the box, until one day it was scared off for good by a glimpse of the contents.

After the canon's death in 1957 the head was buried in the chapel precincts of Sidney Sussex College, Cambridge, where Cromwell had spent a short time as student.

There are other Vansittart-Neale connections to be mentioned. The Edward who added the surname Neale to his former name was twice married, the second time to Anne Spooner (1780–1873). Their great-nephew was the celebrated Reverend William Archibald Spooner (1844–1930) who is remembered for "Spoonerisms," the slip in speech by which the initial letters of words in a phrase are accidentally transposed. A typical and much quoted example is "You will leave Oxford by the next town drain" (down train).

Anne Spooner's sister, Barbara, in 1797 became the wife of William Wilberforce, the evangelical crusader whose work led to the abolition of the slave trade. Another connection must be traced back to Arthur, eldest brother of the Vansittart who bought Bisham Abbey.

That brother had a daughter, Louisa Martha, who in August 1841 married William Chapman of Westmeath, Ireland. Their son, Thomas Robert Tighe Chapman, married a lady who must have been notorious in her time, at least in Ireland, where she was universally known as "the vinegar queen." They had several children but, as her nickname indicates, the marriage was unhappy, and Thomas eventually eloped with the children's governess, a girl named Sara Madan who came from the Isle of Skye.

Thomas Tighe Chapman changed his name to Lawrence, and one of the four sons born to him and Sara Madan was Thomas Edward Lawrence of Arabia who, after organizing the Arab revolt in the desert during World War One, drifted to a somewhat puzzling end as Aircraftman Shaw.

6

The second Vansittart to hold the Abbey was George Henry, grandson of the original purchaser, born at Bisham in 1803. He became M.P. for Berkshire, was twice married but left no son, and died in 1885. He was succeeded by Edward, born in 1810, whose father had adopted the name of Neale.

Educated at Rugby under the celebrated Doctor Arnold, and at Oriel College, Oxford, he became a Chancery barrister of Lincoln's Inn. It therefore seems almost a departure from the tradition of the time to find that he soon fell under the spell of Christian Socialism, then being taught by such men as Robert Owen, who saw co-operation as the answer to the world's growing industrial troubles; Charles Kingsley, cleric and author of *Westward Ho!*, and Broad churchman Frederick Denison Maurice, whose religious and political liberalism was anathema to the orthodox.

Edward's first venture was to start a co-operative building scheme. It ended in failure, he encountered substantial losses, and was forced to sell Allesley Park. But his faith in the movement persisted, as was shown by the number of offices he held within it.

As secretary for the Wholesale Board at Manchester, he lived in that city and travelled to Bisham once weekly. He helped promote the annual congress of co-operators; he was general secretary of the Co-operative Union from 1873 to 1891, and took a leading part in the International Co-operative Alliance.

He gave expression to the evangelical interest that provided a part background to the movement when he published, in 1845, *Feasts and Fasts: an Essay on the rise, progress, and present state of the laws relating to Sundays and other Holidays, and days of Fasting, with notices of the origin of these days, and of the sittings and vacations of the Courts.*

Edward Vansittart-Neale married Frances Sarah, daughter of James Farrer of Ingleborough, Yorkshire, a Master in Chancery; and while living in Kent, in 1864, Edward's daughter Henrietta married Henry, the youngest son of William Dickinson of West Wickham Hall.

When Edward died in 1885 the estate was left to his widow,

Frances Sarah, for life; and on her death in 1894 the succession was vested in Edward's second son, Henry James Vansittart-Neale.

From Eton, where he rowed in the boats (he later rowed from Oxford to Bisham, well over sixty miles, in a day) Henry had gained a competitive appointment in the Admiralty in 1862. Some years later he became assistant-secretary to the Admiralty, was made a C.B. in 1897, and a K.C.B. in 1902. It was the time of Edward VII's coronation, and Henry, on board the royal yacht off Cowes, was concerned with arrangements for the showing of British naval might in the review at Portsmouth.

His wife was Florence, daughter of Judge Arthur Shelly Ellis, Q.C., who for many years was judge at the Clerkenwell County Court. Sir Henry's only son, Kenneth George Vansittart-Neale, died of appendicitis in 1904, at the age of fourteen while a schoolboy at Eton. His monument in the church shows him wearing a Norfolk jacket and ribbed stockings, kneeling at a faldstool with hands clasped over a Bible, and at his feet a favourite dog, Norman.

During the 1914 war the Abbey was a hospital for Belgian soldiers, the dining room and the north bedroom being converted into wards.

Sir Henry died on the 15th of July 1923, and his wife in 1937. Their eldest daughter, Phyllis Mary, continued to live at the Abbey; their second daughter, Elizabeth Frances, married Major Leo Berkeley Paget, M.C., Rifle Brigade, in 1917. Their two sons were killed in the Second World War, Berkeley Henry Vansittart Paget (born 1919) at El Alamein in 1942, and Guy Leo (born 1921) in Italy in 1944. Major Paget died in 1951.

During those war years the Abbey was used as a home for evacuees, and as a billet for troops who formed a special defence battalion for London; while for five years from 1941 it was also a convalescent home for V.A.D. nurses and Red Cross personnel.

After the war Phyllis Mary Vansittart-Neale let the Abbey, at a nominal fee, to the Central Council of Physical Recreation, as a living memorial to her two nephews. The Council there set up the first national recreation centre in the country, and later, with the aid of funds provided by the Government, purchased the Abbey.

Now, as the National Sports Council under the chairmanship of Dr. Roger Bannister, it services national bodies of sport through the promotion of high level coaching and training courses in association football, rugby, hockey, tennis, sailing, archery, and other recreations in line with the sporting traditions of our country.

The English rugby team for 1972, and the Olympic hockey, canoeing, and weight-lifting squads trained at Bisham; and when the present writer last visited the Abbey the blue tracksuits of the Chelsea soccer team were dotting the grass.

When Phyllis Mary died on the 8th January, 1958, the Bisham estate went to her sister, Mrs. Elizabeth Paget, then living at Bisham Grange; and on her death in April, 1965, by reason of Sir Henry Vansittart-Neale's entail to his will, it passed to Mrs. Pamela Thoresby and Miss Margaret Dickinson, the two grandchildren of Sir Henry's sister Henrietta who, as already stated, had married Henry Dickinson in 1864.

During this century there have been four major deaths in the family, each involving high Estate Duties. Now very little of the old manorial estate of the Knights Templars remains intact. The Abbey, the village, and all but one of the farms and a few cottages have been sold; and the village has ceased to be a compact whole united, as once it was, under whichever family was living at "the big house."

The Advowson is still in the hands of Mrs. Thoresby, and the title "Lord of the Manor," very much shorn of its trappings, belongs to Miss Dickinson.

But although the peace that once enveloped Bisham will become, more than ever, a thing of the past with the opening of a new road, the old mansion remains, standing four-square on the banks of the Thames; a monument to the vanished personalities who took their place in the ancient pride and heritage of our land.

PART EIGHT

She Walks by Night

1

The prerequisites that lend an air of historical romance to many great houses—hidden treasure, a secret passage, and a ghost—appear in the story of Bisham Abbey.

Part of the treasure consisted of bags of gold coins, some English, dating from the reigns of Edward III, Henry VIII, Elizabeth I, and Edward VI. Those coins had at some time been secreted under the floor of a small bedroom on the south side of the Abbey, a part of the building that was reconstructed by the Hobys. The hoard was declared to be treasure trove.

But a more mysterious find, and one that cannot be accounted for, was made in 1840. This was a bag of Spanish doubloons, found beneath the floor that serves as cover to the entrance porch, gold coins that were minted, since they bore the heads of King Ferdinand and Queen Isabella, in the mid-15th century.

Speculation runs rife when trying to account for the appearance of the coins at the Abbey. Had some adventurous guest of the Hobys been one of a party of English seamen who stormed their way aboard a great floating castle of Spain, and did the coins represent his share of the treasure found in its hold? Or is there some possible connection between the find and the fact that the Lovelace family, of nearby Ladye Place, owed their fortune to a piratical venture on the Spanish main?

Further discoveries, of an equally puzzling nature, consisted of a set of baby clothes and a pair of infant's gloves. Of fine linen and point lace, their appearance is startlingly fresh.

There are also articles that have been identified as being part of the clothing worn by a boy bishop.

The appointment of a boy bishop was a curious feature of medieval religion. On St. Nicholas's day, December the 6th, the choir boys in cathedral churches chose one of their number to take on the position of a bishop, which meant that he could perform all ecclesiastical ceremonies with the exception of Mass. During his time of office, which expired on December the 28th, he was habited in the usual ecclesiastical clothes and vestments. The ceremony was abrogated in 1542. It was revived for a time, and then only to the extent of dressing a boy bishop to figure in processions in the London diocese, during the reign of Catholic Mary.

Since the ceremony took place only in cathedral churches, it cannot have occurred at Bisham; and here again one can merely speculate—was Blessed Margaret of Salisbury, the mother of Cardinal Pole, in some way responsible for bringing the boy bishop's clothes to her riverside home?

A reminder of the Austin Canons' tenure at Bisham came to light with the discovery of a stone coffin, which held two keys and some human bones. The presence of the keys points to the fact that the remains were those of a religious superior, possibly the prior, who had been responsible for the safe keeping and order of the house. The bones were re-buried in the hall, and the cover of the coffin now rests against a wall near the cloister.

The secret room was originally reached by way of the great fireplace in one of the bedrooms; but now the narrow stairs ascending to it are revealed by moving a piece of furniture. The stairs lead to what is virtually a miniature hall, with fine oak rafters. Life at the Abbey was predominantly peaceful, but the room was probably constructed in Tudor times when the expression or even the holding of a political or religious opinion might be fraught with danger.

An air of secrecy also attached to an underground passage, which runs from the right hand side of a window in the gun-room along the south side of the Abbey towards the river. Built of brick, with a rounded roof, there are spaces where it is possible for one to stand upright. Although blocked up for a time, an investigation carried out by police frogmen in 1957 confirmed the long-held belief that the passage found an outlet in the river.

A last word on the Bisham tapestries—it was decided to treat them, during the Vansittart-Neale occupation, to what was blandly described, by those who carried it out, as a cleaning and mending process.

The process, which went on at intervals for months, consisted of the tapestries being spread on the lawn and doused with buckets of water. But such was 16th century workmanship that the tapestries miraculously survived. After this the many pieces were sent to the Victoria and Albert Museum, where they were pieced together before being hung in all their ancient glory in the Great Hall. They were ultimately purchased by Lord Gort on behalf of the Irish Republic, and are now housed in Bunratty Castle, near Shannon.

The list of royal visitors to the Abbey can be extended to include the following names:

Queen Victoria. She did no more than "call." For the message informing the Vansittart-Neales of her approach apparently went astray. When the Queen's carriage arrived at the entrance the family was out, and to make matters worse the footman fumbled and seemed unable to find the bell. The horses were turned about, and the indignant "Widow of Windsor," settling stiffly back in her carriage, never came that way again.

Edward VII, as Prince of Wales, was sometimes entertained at the Abbey during his frequent visits to General Owen Williams at Temple House.

Before their marriage, George V and Queen Mary were guests at a house-party given at the Abbey. Their daughter Mary, the Princess Royal, was also a visitor.

The Duke of York (the future George VI) and the Duchess of York.

Princess Marina of Kent.

Prince Paul of Yugoslavia.

The Duke of Edinburgh, who in June 1956 arrived by

helicopter at the Abbey in his capacity as President of the Council of Physical Recreation.

2

Some investigators who have studied the subject of ghosts refer to Bisham Abbey as being one of the most haunted houses in England; and judging by portraits of the dead who are said to visit their former homes, no one is better fitted or more likely to cast a sinister influence over the walls that once reflected their shadow than Lady Hoby.

Her portrait shows her dressed in black, doubtless as a sign of mourning for her perfect husband Thomas. But there is no sign of mourning in her face. Her features, especially the eyes, and even the general set of her face under her wimple, proclaim that here was a woman of no uncertain quality, but of such cold calculation and interest as to leave her without mercy, without a sign of seeking or accepting surrender; and even if the face were blotted out, her hands, thin and white as though no blood had ever passed through them, would seem to belie their delicacy and take on the character of talons.

The story of "wicked Lady Hoby" has found various levels of interpretation. She was once the subject of local gossip, which is now dying out. It used to be highly dangerous to penetrate the mist that on autumn evenings veils the Abbey frontage and the opposite bank of the river. The mist was held to be a swirling menace, inspired by the lady, that could lead, beyond all efforts of will power, to drowning.

Two boys, passing between the Abbey and the church after a fishing expedition, saw in the twilight a boat drawn up by the bank. In it sat a woman, whom they took to be old. She was hooded, dressed in black, a figure brooding and mysterious as the mist that shredded about the silent boat on the motionless water.

Other stories concerned a light that was sometimes seen, from across the river, burning in the tower room when it was empty; unseen hands that in the dead of night plucked off bedclothes; the door of the library that, after being closed, would suddenly spring open of its own accord; while the most puzzling local legend, that has no bearing on any recorded incident, was to the effect that Lady Hoby had fed her children on the leg of a lark.

But most persistent stories, that cannot be connected with any known fabricator, have some grounding in fact, however distantly that fact and the legend may seem to be related; and the fact that emerges with the verity that sustains much commonly accepted history is that Lady Hoby, with her own hands or through negligence, brought about the death of one of her own sons.

Her reason for doing so corresponds with what we know of her character, and her passion for scholarship. It was by no means unusual for well established families, at that time, to have the same regard for the educational standards of their children as now most parents have for their material advancement; the household of Sir Thomas More at Chelsea, like that of the Cookes at Gidea Park where Lady Hoby developed, are paramount examples; while Lady Jane Grey, looking back down the shortening avenue of her own young life, records that she sometimes fancied herself in hell because of the "pinches, nips and bobs" inflicted upon her when she faltered over some exercise.

But Lady Hoby (and her portrait would seem to bear this out) was of a more violent nature than either of Jane's parents. The name of the boy victim is usually given as William, and Lady Hoby is said to have beaten him to death when, during a writing lesson in one of the tower rooms, he smudged or dropped ink upon his books, or proved inordinately backward.

Another account says that she dealt him a fatal blow with a heavy ruler. A more unlikely and less authenticated version is that his irregular writing so angered his mother that she tied him to a chair and left him alone to make an improved copy.

To dissipate her resentment she went riding in Bisham woods, where she met Queen Elizabeth who invited her back to Windsor. She went, without a thought for the boy whose plight was unknown to the servants; and when she returned she found him dead, still tied to the chair.

A slightly different slant is given to the story by mention of a kind of bower that was built on the edge of the lawn, near the river, and used as a schoolroom. There, in full view of villagers on the towpath opposite, she was seen ill treating the hapless boy; and one gossip related in a nearby inn (was it the "Bull"?) that he had seen "my lady's boy" being beaten about the head till he collapsed with blood streaming from his eyes, nose and mouth, and saturating the grass.

It would seem, however, that the irascible dowager acquired a somewhat gentler cast of character after her transfer to the Bisham vault. For her ghost, according to some who claim to have encountered her in a bedroom, on the tower stairs, approaching the library, or in the grounds, walks in a sorrowful or repentant mood, as did Lady Macbeth, with a bowl of invisible water floating before her, and into which she dips her hands in a vain effort to wash away the stain or remembrance of guilt.

She has, moreover, the uncanny habit of materialising in the negative, or in reverse, with her dress that is known to have been black appearing white, and the headdress, collar and cuffs showing black instead of white.

But the identity or even the existence of a young William Hoby, or Russell, has never been established. There is no entry of his birth in the Bisham parish register; and the absence of positive evidence in that respect provides an excuse for some who dislike any mention of the supernatural to reject the whole story as false.

But such reasoning is faulty. The absence of written record is not a decisive factor in forming a judgment, historical or otherwise. The Hobys were not limited to the Bisham house; the boy's birth could have been registered elsewhere, apart from which people of influence could have had all trace of it removed when the tragedy occurred.

A woman of Lady Hoby's character would have thought herself sufficiently punished by having to acknowledge one of her sons, Thomas Posthumous, as a disappointing failure; and her relatives might well have connived at obscuring all mention of a second source of shame in the backward William, so that his violent and unnatural death remained a close secret with the family.

At any rate a discovery made much later, in 1840, adds a realistic touch to the traditional story and weakens the case of those who dismiss it as fable. During the course of structural alterations, when part of the dining room floor was taken up, a corner near the window gave way. A quantity of rubble mixed with old papers was revealed, and on this being cleared some faded copy books were found between the joists of the floor.

Next day Mrs. Vansittart, who was there at the time, examined the copy books. She found that they contained signatures of the Hoby family, together with a number of corrections made by Lady Hoby. Mrs. Vansittart goes on to say: "In one of William Hoby, I think, every leaf had some blot . . . I wanted to take two or three away with me that day, but my sister-in-law wished to keep them till Admiral Henry Vansittart had examined them. When I asked for them all were missing, they suddenly had disappeared, supposed to be sold by the workmen."

Two clothes-baskets had been used to carry away the litter; and with it went the evidence that might have confirmed the old unhappy story of an irate mother and a boy who was careless or too dull to learn.

3

A fact to be noted about the Bisham manifestations is that the supernatural there reveals itself in a number of different ways. One of the most direct and striking testimonies, as regards the actual appearance of Lady Hoby, comes from Admiral Edward W. Vansittart, who was born at Bisham Grange and died at the age of eighty-six in 1904. As the son of Henry Vansittart, Vice-Admiral of the Blue, he was the second member of the family to reach high naval rank.

The Admiral relates how he was sitting up late one night with his brother, over a game of chess, in a panelled room overlooked by the portrait of Lady Hoby. "We had finished playing, and my brother had gone up to bed. I stood for some time with my back to the wall, turning over the day in my mind. Minutes passed. I suddenly realised the presence of someone standing behind me. I tore round. It was Dame Hoby. The frame on the wall was empty. Terrified, I fled the room."

The Admiral's record is one that hardly leaves him open to the charge of instability or of being preyed on by nervous fancy. He was active in naval operations in the Persian Gulf, and took a prominent part in the suppression of Chinese piracy. On one occasion he destroyed a fleet of forty war junks, and lived up to the typical traditions of knight-errantry plus service by rescuing a party of English ladies from a pirate stronghold.

Sir George Grove, one time director of the Royal College of Music, and editor of the standard *Dictionary of Music and Musicians,* refers in one of his notebooks, dated 1880, to the experience of a Foreign Office clerk who was invited to a ball at the Abbey.

On arrival, he was told that a room had been arranged for him at the local inn. The visitor expressed a wish to spend the night at the Abbey, but his host explained that the only room available was the green room.

"Well, what is the green room?" asked the visitor.

"It's an odd room that is never slept in; indeed, they say it is haunted."

The visitor, who had brought his dog, said that he would not mind the ghost if he could have his retriever in the bedroom.

It was a high room with a bright fire burning in the big fireplace, and a very tall old bed. The visitor was soon asleep, but something roused him. The fire had died down to a glimmer, and suddenly he heard what he could only describe as a drop falling, "a thick sort of sound not like water."

The sound was followed by another and then another. The drops came nearer, until they seemed to be falling on a strip of carpet at the foot of the bed. The dog, which had been padding about the room, leapt up and snuggled, quivering, against the now equally alarmed listener, who felt a cold mist was creeping over him. Then he fainted. In the morning he was so ashamed that he availed himself of the earliest chance to leave the Abbey.

The present writer, who spent a night in the haunted room at the Abbey, was not, somewhat to his relief, favoured by a visit from Lady Hoby. But it was otherwise with a lusty young man who, during a crowded house-party at the time of one Henley Regatta, where he was competing, was given a shakedown in the Abbey library. The young man, who had a fine head of curly hair of which he was justly proud, was obviously put out and in a state of nerves when he appeared at breakfast.

On being pressed for an explanation he told how Lady Hoby had approached him, and raising one of her attenuated hands had spoken words that showed an understanding of his little foible: "Young man, if I but touch thee, thou wilt be bald." A note of sincerity is added to the story when we learn that the young man, besides giving up rowing, went into the Church.

A book entitled *No Alibi*, by Captain Alastair Mackintosh, again treats of a party given at Bisham Abbey. It was during the First World War, and among the guests was a certain Adeline Drysdale. The latter retired early one night when a small informal dance was in progress, and suddenly she surprised the dancers by rushing downstairs, wild-eyed and terrified.

According to her story she was reading a book, with her West Highland terrier on the bed (a curtained four-poster) when the door opened. The dog, its hackles up, jumped off the bed and ran out of the room. Adeline's diamond wrist-watch was then lifted from the side table on which she had placed it, and flung in a corner. The toilet set was then knocked over, a pile of music was thrown onto the floor, and unseen hands roughly tore down the curtains of the bed.

The figure of a tall woman was seen to be standing between the bed-posts, wearing a white garment that, Adeline said, might have been an old fashioned nightdress. Adeline was afterwards asked to examine the portraits in the dining room, and without hesitation she recognised Lady Hoby as having been the intruder. Apart from that experience, says Captain Mackintosh, "we often heard the most awful noises coming from behind the panelling in the hall."

More recent testimony is provided by Mrs. Anne Palmer, who worked with the V.A.D. at the Abbey during World War II. She was on late duty one night, preparing a fermentation for a patient who was sleeping out in the cloisters, when she heard a loud sobbing. It seemed to come from the hall, but after passing through the hall and along a passage leading out to the cloisters, she found that her charge was sitting up in bed, quite cheerful and without the trace of a tear.

All was quiet in the wards. Mrs. Palmer was not alarmed then, merely puzzled. But, she says, "on looking back, I can't think why my bags weren't packed the next morning and I was away in a cloud of dust." For she later realised that no sound of sobbing could have been heard through the thick walls of the Abbey, even had a living person been there.

Another night found Mrs. Palmer on duty in what was known as the Red Room. There was a good fire, the room was well lighted, and after disposing of her tasks she settled down for a rest. But after a few minutes she became aware of a most uncomfortable sensation.

She was being stared at, fixedly, by someone who was quietly watching . . . watching . . . After a time she could bear the silent scrutiny no longer and withdrew to the kitchens. Never again did she pass a moment's leisure in the Red Room.

Perhaps the eyes that discomforted her on that occasion had not wept those many years ago when the deed that was to call them out of the darkness had been perpetrated.

*　　*　　*　　*　　*

Its walls take on the colour of the changing seasons. Birds circle above the dark trees that make a shadowy frame for its pointed gables and mullioned windows.

A group of visitors pause on the river bank. One acts vaguely as guide. "It's called an Abbey, so the monks were there."

The evening light wears down from the Chilterns and veils both commentator and the Abbey. But tomorrow the place will come to life and make physical demands on those who seek to be expert at games, and whose shoes patter, as they serve or return a ball at tennis, over the dust of the man who made Kings and of Earls who stood at bay on the fields of Crécy and Agincourt.

Index